THE EDUCATOR'S

GUIDE TO CHILD
UNDERSTANDING DEVELOPMENT

Supporting Healthy Academic and Emotional Growth

THE EDUCATOR'S

GUIDE TO UNDERSTANDING CHILD DEVELOPMENT

Supporting Healthy Academic and Emotional Growth

LINDA C. MAYES, M.D.

◨SCHOLASTIC

YALE CHILD STUDY CENTER+
SCHOLASTIC COLLABORATIVE
for Child & Family Resilience

Portions of this book were previously published in *The Yale Child Study Center Guide to Understanding Your Child: Healthy Development From Birth to Adolescence* by Linda C. Mayes, M.D. and Donald J. Cohen, M.D. with John E. Schowalter, M.D. and Richard H. Granger, M.D.

ISBN 978-1-338-78785-6

1 2 3 4 5 6 7 8 9 10   40   30 29 28 27 26 25 24 23 22 21

Scholastic Inc., 557 Broadway, New York, NY 10012

This book is dedicated to all the teachers who gave me so much of themselves—their time and caring. They imagined who I could be and helped me to get there. Thank you to Dixie Vaughan, Ruth Arnold, Mary Parker, Jerry Smith, and so many more.

Acknowledgements

The Yale Child Study Center Guide to Understanding Your Child was first published in 2001 as a comprehensive text for parents. The book was conceived not just to provide information about children's developmental milestones but also as a guide for adults in their own development as they become parents. Letting another person into our minds as we care for them is a profound human endeavor that changes each of us along the way at every level of our being from brain to mind. Being a parent is one path to that change but so is being a teacher. When we assume the responsibility of teaching children, we not only take on the task of conveying knowledge and skills; we also become their guide—imagining who they can be, their better selves, their fullest potential. To be able to do this with a child is a multigenerational gift—for the child and for the adult. Giving of ourselves to others—as teachers do every day—transforms us.

The original book had many contributors who brought their perspectives and ideas to the text. Among those were a coauthor and two consulting colleagues. Donald J. Cohen, a child psychiatrist and director of the Child Study Center at the time of the book's publication, had a near intuitive capacity to reach children and bring out their inner lives. Dr. Cohen and I worked closely and in the original version was a coauthor of the book. Dr. Richard Granger, a consultant to the original book, was a developmental pediatrician and another close colleague of mine. He too was able to be deeply in touch with the children he saw in his practice. He used his encyclopedic memory of Broadway songs to help children feel at ease—humming a tune or even teaching a shy or anxious child a short Cole Porter lyric as he examined them. Years later, those children as adults would remember his songs or the evenings he made a house call when they were sick. Their parents felt cared for too by his always keeping their needs in mind. And Dr. John Schowalter, another child psychiatrist and consultant to the original book, brought his expertise in adolescents. Dr. Schowalter has a wickedly good sense of irony and humor that especially engaged adolescents and emerging young adults and allowed him to meet the young person where they most needed him. Additionally, there were many other colleagues who contributed their clinical insights and years of experience working with families to ground the text in real world stories.

Adapting and updating the original text for a new audience and the educational setting has been an exciting project of the Yale Child Study Center–Scholastic Collaborative for Child and Family Resilience. Karen Baicker has led this effort from Scholastic and her partnership in the adaptation and writing has been a gift. Karen ably leads the Collaborative with her creativity as a writer and artist. She is also a gifted children's book author who always connects compassionately with children. It is a special honor to have her as a colleague.

Introduction

The fundamental tasks of child rearing—its joys, its worries, its aims— lie within families. However, to achieve this vital human role, parents have for millennia looked to society as a guide and for support. It is only relatively recently—owing to the many advances in science and psychology of the 20th century—that parents in Western society began to consider each child as an individual with his or her own patterns and processes of development. As a result, parents held themselves responsible both for fostering their child's development in accordance with his or her personal needs and for helping him or her grow up to function as a productive and responsible member of society.

As teachers today, you are at the forefront of two contemporary arcs of thought: each child is an individual who will develop, with family support, along a unique path; and child development is the collective responsibility of society. Teachers, neighbors, friends, social workers and community members can all play a vital role in helping children grow into their happiest and most successful selves.

This book was developed as a project of the Yale Child Study Center–Scholastic Collaborative for Child and Family Resilience. The mission of the Collaborative is to foster the intersection of literacy and mental health and to deepen practices that help build resilience in children, families and communities. This book has been adapted from the authoritative book for parents, *The Yale Child Study Center Guide to Understanding Your Child*.

Our goal is to give educators the background knowledge and insights behind the alchemy by which an infant transforms into the child who graces your classroom, bursting with personality. *The Educator's Guide to Understanding Child Development* seeks not only to help you understand each child and his or her development from birth but also goes further to explore how you support their parents and understand yourself as a teacher. The insights from this book will help inform your teaching practice as you gain greater knowledge of a child's cognitive and emotional development.

Since 1911, the Yale Child Study Center has been at the forefront both of the scientific study of infants and children and of the use of developmental knowledge to provide guidance to parents, educators, and professionals. Research conducted in the Center has helped shape our modern understanding of children and their lives. Today the Yale Child Study Center is a source for creative collaboration among experts in child and adolescent psychiatry, psychology, social work, pediatrics, education, neuroscience, nursing, human genetics, and law. The faculty connects with a wider public through their work with national and international media, government agencies, and public and private child- and family-advocacy organizations.

Some families come to the Center because they have developmental, behavioral, or family troubles; others, to participate in studies of psychological and neurological development. The Center has worked with thousands of families over the years: today we see the grandchildren of adults who came to the Center during its earliest years.

We have met thousands of parents and children in our cumulative years of practice. The stories we have gathered from these families— parents and children from all walks of life who relate in different ways— deeply inform our developmental approach to, and understanding of, parenting and childhood. Through the situations these families encounter—their best and worst moments, joys and worries, triumphs and disappointments—we trace what it means to be a child, raise a child, teach a child. Not every story we tell represents a single family; some are combinations of experiences. We combine stories with observation, the practical with the theoretical.

In this book we speak from three perspectives: the most up-to-date knowledge of the science of child development; a child's point of view at particular ages and stages of development; and adults' expectations and experience of that development.

From the first perspective—the scientific one—we discuss the most basic needs adults must meet: helping babies sleep, finding the most developmentally engaging toys for infants and toddlers, managing aggression, and understanding how children learn.

In offering information or suggesting ways to think about a difficult situation or handle normal concerns, we also emphasize that knowledge alone is not sufficient. Thus, from the second perspective, you must balance facts with an understanding of each child's feelings. Appreciating how a two-year-old understands feelings and ordinary day-to-day circumstances differently from a five-year-old helps you navigate the rapidly changing development of a young child.

Finally, to balance facts and understanding children's feelings, you must also be aware of and allow for the inner life of the adults who care for children as parents and as teachers. This all-important third perspective makes this book unique. For those feelings—what you imagine and hope for children—are as important as what you do or say, if not more so. This third perspective is also about making room for children in your mind and in your life. Each child you reach lives within your mind long after she leaves your classroom. Similarly, the impact that you make on that child will stay not only with the child but will ripple out into the community and into future generations.

A child develops through forward leaps, plateaus, even steps backward. As much as you may like to think of children as moving ahead all the time, you will often need to pause and even revisit developmental stages. From time to time, in keeping with this point of view, we may repeat ourselves to remind you that even as development moves forward, familiar themes will pop up again and again.

Just as you—as a teacher and perhaps a parent yourself—are the endpoint of countless generations, so the children you teach are the beginning of generations to come. They need your protection as well as your guidance. Raising children is never an easy endeavor; it is often lonely, rarely predictable, sometimes frightening. Often parents feel overwhelmed with seemingly unanswerable problems and questions. The more you understand about the journey of children and the adults who love them, the more support you can give.

Contents

CHAPTER I

Understanding Child Development

A brief grounding in the history of the field of child development will help you understand the mysterious alchemy by which an infant morphs changes into a fully formed person.

A two-year-old is different from a young adult. Both are different from newborns. "Of course," you may reply, "of course, children don't look, behave, or think like adults. "Of course, something turns babies into adults physically and mentally." When you chide a friend or colleague for being "childish," you are implicitly acknowledging the process whereby an unruly child changes into a mature adult capable of accepting responsibilities and behaving appropriately. Through a mysterious, unpredictable process that is sometimes even a bit frightening, the infants we welcome into the world will someday become a student, a classmate a young worker, and even a parent. This is the process we have come to call "child development."

Most people today probably understand that a child's body, behavior, and mind mature according to various biological and genetic programs. Research has also found that just as an engine needs fuel, a child needs to have certain experiences for these programs to run properly. But experience is just part of the picture; clearly, children do not become adults through their experiences alone. The process isn't something one can orchestrate: we cannot teach our four-year-olds to think and behave completely like adults, or stop a twelve-year-old from becoming an adolescent. These important changes occur according to a timetable that is influenced, but not controlled, by outside events. Development thus involves a complex interplay of genes, other biological factors, and experience. As educators we are trusted, critical adults who can help nurture this developmental process.

Developing the Idea of Human Development

Until late in the eighteenth century, children in Western society were viewed as essentially small, untutored adults. Every characteristic of an adult was thought to be present, however indistinctly, from birth. What separated the child from the adult was mostly size and knowledge. Though children legally remained minors until they were twenty-one or so, most entered the working world when they were still children. Culturally, children were thought of as small adults. In factories, child labor was not only accepted, it was preferred. Children were small which made it easy for them to get into small parts of the machines.

Until relatively recently, children were thought to function like adults in small bodies, to think like adults who lacked sufficient experience and teaching, and to behave like adults without the benefits of socialization into their communities and cultures.

In the late nineteenth century, scientific research into prenatal development began to change that view. Careful study of fetuses revealed for the first time that their physical development occurs in stages, with forms and organs emerging gradually. The fetus is not, in fact, a fully shaped little human who simply gets bigger. These findings were followed in the early twentieth century by the discovery that after birth, hormones in the body produce a series of physical changes, including growth and puberty.

This notion of gradual, lifelong physical development set the stage for the idea that humans also undergo a psychological development that defines and shapes one's abilities.

The concept of emerging abilities was applied to mental and behavioral development by the early 1920s, when psychologists, teachers, and physicians began to map out the stages of mental growth. By the middle of the twentieth century, the basic foundations of child development were widely accepted, and scholars turned their attention to the ways in which a child's thinking differs from an adult's. The Swiss psychologist Jean Piaget (1896–1980) made the radical proposal that children's approaches to their surroundings appear illogical only if one assumes that their minds function as adults' do. Based on his research, he concluded that children make sense of their world using a series of thought processes that have their own logic—thought processes that appear in a regular order, each characteristic of a particular age. (See pages 6–7.) In mapping out children's progression through these different ways of understanding the world, Piaget provided a new window on how children learn and how their minds develop a variety of capabilities for learning and understanding.

As the Second World War spread across Europe, clinicians caring for war orphans applied a similar developmental approach to understanding children's emotional development. Anna Freud, among others, discovered that just as children have their own order and logic for understanding the inanimate world, their capacity to understand their emotional world develops through a standard series of stages. The emotional skills required to understand their own feelings and the feelings of others, to cope with disappointment and sadness, and to care for their own bodies and needs emerge over the course of early childhood. (See Chapters 8–9 for more on emotional development.) Researchers trying to understand the emotional life of children also called attention to the importance of a child's emerging capacity for imaginative play.

Researchers recognized that far from being "child's play," imaginative play is an important way station in a child's ability to try out, practice, and master various emotions and experiences.

The years since have provided much more scientific evidence to support this modern view of child development. In this view, children travel, both chronologically and developmentally, across a complex web of developmental pathways in different sequences and at different paces. This passage is influenced by a variety of factors.

Nature or Nurture—or Both?

The discovery that a child's mental, motor, and emotional skills unfold along a more or less regular timeline made scientists think, at first, that all development proceeded in ordered stages regulated by a biological clock. In this view, while children might vary in how early or late they reach a stage, the majority, pushed along by their biology, ultimately move through each stage on a path to adulthood. Researchers later revised this maturational theory of development by suggesting that a child's experiences shape how quickly he approaches each developmental stage and how well he masters what is most important during that stage. For example, children who grow up with little language stimulation may be slower to begin using language and to learn the language skills they will need for subsequent stages of development.

The contrast between these different approaches to development is captured in the debate between nature and nurture. How much does biology contribute to children's maturation? How much do experiences? The pendulum has swung from a mid-twentieth-century preference for nurture—in which almost every aspect of a person's behavior is ascribed to his early childhood experiences (especially, critics have written, to how he was treated by his mother)—to the more current preference for discovering biochemical or genetic roots for a range of behaviors and conditions. Some scientists even claim that a child's genes influence her future behavior and health more powerfully than her experiences do.

Most of us, however, see a mix of causes. Contemporary theories of development do not make either nature or nurture primary. Each is seen to influence the other. The current understanding of child development embraces the idea of gene-environment interaction. Genes provide the individual blueprint for a child: blue eyes, brown hair, tall or short, athletic or musical or both. But genes are not simply set in motion in the fetus or newborn, playing out like a movie from beginning to end: experience plays a vital role in much of a child's development.

Particular experiences may be critical for some genes to turn on (that is, to become active and express their genetic code) and allow capacities to develop. For example, for the full connections to the visual centers of the brain to develop, the eye must be stimulated by light. Movement and muscle stimulation are required for muscles to grow. Good nutrition or language stimulation enrich the expression of genes into a person's full potential. An event early in development may continue to influence many later events, including the later expression of genes. Thus, if a young child experiences serious illness, malnutrition, or overwhelming stress, the effects of those long-past events may delay the onset of puberty when she reaches her teens.

An infant's brain and body are genetically set to respond to his environment, and genes provide the structure for the gradual, timed unfolding of the central nervous system in fetal and postnatal life. But each child's experiences, provided at first by those who love and care for him, "switch on" critical processes in his central nervous system that prepare him to make use of the attention that caring adults provide. The earliest interactions between a baby's genetically timed biological systems and her environment have an effect on *both* her brain and her behavior.

Learning as a Two-Step Process

Piaget concluded that children (and adults) learn in a two-step process. Upon encountering something new, a child first considers how it is similar to what he already knows. By this method, he fits new experiences into the picture of the world that he has in his mind. Piaget called this step, whereby one notes how a new thing is similar to familiar things, *assimilation*.

Eventually, however, a child encounters phenomena, people, or objects that she cannot fit into her worldview, or realizes that her initial assumption that something is familiar proves not to be the case. For instance, a preschooler may decide that she can play with the ball she found in the sandbox because it is a toy like those she has at home. But as soon as a bigger child comes to take his ball back, she realizes that something was wrong with that conclusion. Faced with this discrepancy, she takes the next step in learning: she changes her thinking to *accommodate reality*. Children and adults follow these two steps continually throughout their lives and, in doing so, gradually add to and refine their knowledge of how the world really works.

The Main Stages of Cognitive Development

Jean Piaget was one of the first scholars to study systematically how children learn. Over the course of his career, he pioneered several new scientific fields, including developmental psychology and cognitive theory. Although Piaget started his career as a zoologist studying mollusks, he later moved to Paris to study logic and abnormal psychology. Working with Alfred Binet, a pioneering researcher on intelligence and the codeveloper of an important standard IQ test, Piaget studied the way young children approach intelligence tests, and wanted to find out whether there are patterns to the mistakes they commonly make.

Based on many years of observing how children of different ages conceive of physical reality, numbers, and morality, Piaget posited that there are four main stages of cognitive development:

- The **sensorimotor** stage lasts on average from birth to about age two. In this stage, a baby learns through his movements and senses, especially hearing, sight, and feeling with his hands and mouth. He identifies the boundary between his body and the rest of the world, and learns which basic sensations and feelings are connected to which events around him. Early on, babies can identify simple goals and work toward them. Toward the end of this stage, babies grasp what Piaget called "object permanence": the knowledge that an object is still around even when he cannot see it. A baby in his first year will not look for a toy if something blocks his sight of it. After eighteen months or so, not only does he know the toy is still there, but he also loves playing with this new knowledge.

- The **preoperational stage** generally lasts from two to seven years old. Young children in this stage start to work with symbols, using words, letters, numbers, and toys to represent concepts. They begin to use simple rules, classifications, and logic to organize their picture of the world, although these rules are often simplistic. For example, children of this age commonly assume that a tall glass must contain more milk than a short, wide glass, and that books spread all over the floor must be more numerous than books shelved together. They still have some difficulty seeing another person's point of view.

- The **concrete operational stage** lasts from seven to eleven years of age, on average. In these years, children's logical abilities grow much more powerful, especially when they tackle concrete or hands-on challenges. They understand how to think backward from their goal in order to figure out how to do what they want to do. Among the more difficult concepts that children grasp in these years is how time works, how "more" can mean different things in different situations, and how two people can view the same event from different perspectives.

- The formal **operational stage** starts around age eleven and lasts through adulthood. Preteens and young adolescents are finally able to master many types of abstract thinking: hypothetical situations; analyses that involve multiple points of view and sets of values; complex mathematical, linguistic, or scientific functions. This capacity leads them to think more about social issues, justice and fairness, and their own place in society.

While subsequent generations of child developmentalists have augmented and revised Piaget's ideas, we still rely on many of his observations and insights about children, particularly his ideas that children of different ages simply understand the world differently—not because they know less but because their minds function differently.

Principles for Understanding Development

As you observe and participate in the process of a child's development, keep in mind the following principles: at any one landmark, there is a great deal of revision and adaptation; each child is unique and does not necessarily develop at the same pace as any other; and a child's progress is, in part, a process of maintaining harmony and synchrony among what is happening in various areas of development.

Revision and Adaptation

When we talk about development, we do not mean simply that a child is always growing bigger, stronger, smarter, more articulate, and more agile and adding new skills on top of others. Certainly, if all goes well, this does happen. But central to the development of any skill or competence are the linked processes of revision and adaptation. In the first process, a child revises functions, skills, even behaviors as necessary. New skills borrow from old ones, and children will weave old skills into new capabilities, so that what was once a skill unto itself is no longer as distinct or recognizable. For example, a newborn's sucking reflex is subsumed into the many other skills of biting, chewing, and sipping that a child needs to eat. (See Chapter 3 for more about feeding.)

The skills a child develops first are not necessarily just primitive versions of his later skills. In some cases, infants actually lose early capacities as they develop. Infants are born, for instance, with the ability to recognize many more sounds than appear in any single language, but each infant gradually comes to distinguish only those sounds her family uses to communicate. (See Chapter 5.) Babies give up crawling for walking, but once they become competent walkers, they are never again so competent at crawling. A baby can still crawl, but he is less facile and less likely to choose that form of locomotion over walking no matter how competent a crawler he was. The muscle actions a child uses for crawling are programmed in the brain; as those actions adapt to walking, the brain program is revised. A new skill has emerged and replaced an old one. Development is thus like remodeling an old home. Vestiges of the old are woven into the new; eighteenth century beams hold up a twenty-first century roof.

Development also means that some abilities and even behaviors are more prominent at ages when a child most needs them to adapt to his environment and are more obscure at later ages. Newborns are

"prewired" to pay attention to special kinds of information—those bits and pieces of data about the adults who take care of them. An infant is especially alert to the rhythms of speech, to the contours and boundaries of a face, and to the smells of her mother and father. These special capacities are present from the first hours of life, even before experience brings them out. As each baby grows, however, her sensory radar for details that signal the presence of important adults becomes woven into more complex abilities. These include being able to play such games as peekaboo, to remember caregivers when they are not present, and ultimately to imagine happy moments. The infant's basic attentiveness to smells, sounds, and touch thus becomes a small part of a more complicated repertoire. A new set of abilities has emerged and incorporated the earlier, basic ones.

You have probably sometimes had the sensation of reliving something you remember deeply from your infancy—perhaps a smell in the air, snatches of a song, an old, worn, soft toy or blanket. You cannot quite call up a specific incident or story, but you feel a wave of emotions: comfort, longing, even sadness. These memories most often happen with tiny bits of sensation—seeing, hearing, smelling, touching. They may well be the vestiges of your earliest abilities to perceive especially well those bits of the world most connected to your childhood.

Adaptation is another key aspect of children's development. At each stage of development, children acquire, practice, and master the skills that are most useful to them at that time. For example, after children learn to walk and run, they can go greater distances from their parents. Developing language in the same months gives a youngster a way to stay in touch: she can call out to Daddy in the backyard as she walks away to look at a neighbor's kitten. At the same time, children of this age are more emotionally sensitive to separations. They practice games of hide-and-seek, coming and going. (See Chapter 7 on helping children deal with separation.) Each of these developmental phases and skills is adapted to the child's current overarching concern: how to stay safe and protected even as she moves physically apart from her parents. As she masters those tasks, she can move on to the next challenges: caring for her own body, dressing and feeding herself, telling stories about what she did when her parents were not there to watch. As she gets older, hide-and-seek becomes a game to play with her friends. Then it becomes a "baby game" she no longer plays, even as she uses the same skills to locate the outfit she plans to wear the next day. What is adaptive at one developmental phase may be less appropriate or less necessary at another.

Variability Among Children

The second principle underlying the idea of development is that every child is different. As an educator, this is a reality you see first-hand every day. None follows a map precisely, nor does every area of development adhere to the same timetable. One child may walk earlier than another or use words a few months later. A child may skip crawling and instead stand and walk with support. He may be precocious in his language development but slow to learn how to dress himself or to tolerate frustration.

Not only is there great variability in how and when individual children achieve developmental milestones, there are also variations in how each child moves up and down these developmental ladders. Newly gained skills such as language are sensitive to stress, and often a gain in one area is matched by a loss or slowing in another. For example, a child learning to walk independently may for a few weeks add no new words to his vocabulary. Newly gained skills such as language are sensitive to stress, and a toddler who has just learned to talk when she develops pneumonia or loses her beloved nanny may stop talking for days or weeks. Or a young child who has mastered going to the toilet on his own may begin wetting himself again when his family moves to a new home some distance from his beloved grandparents.

Children simultaneously proceed along several paths of development, not just one. Generally, experts recognize the areas of physical, cognitive (learning), social, and emotional development, but there are many variations even within these categories. Abilities from different areas are often interrelated, as walking and talking are; sometimes it is difficult to proceed along one pathway without having developed certain skills in another area. Yet each child moves along these developmental roads at his own pace. This explains how a bright student can also be socially immature—mental and social skills are different. A child who can remember dozens of sports statistics can forget to send her grandmother a thank-you letter, and a young bodybuilder may seem unable to lift a laundry basket up the stairs.

In sum, development is not always linear, stable, or consistent. Gains may be accompanied by temporary losses, and children may leapfrog over one milestone to reach another. Models showing development from birth to young adulthood are usually on target for the whole population of children, but do not necessarily predict the route any individual child will take. Developing in different areas at different times is part of what makes each child unique.

Harmony and Progress

Finally, typical development involves both harmony and integration, and normal elaboration and progress: that is, how evenly matched is a child's development in various areas of competence? Are his motor skills, say, far more advanced than his language skills, or are both progressing at a more or less similar pace?

When psychiatrists and other experts assess a child's development, this expectation of harmony helps them determine whether a particular behavior—or lack of it—is relatively normal or seriously discrepant. During an assessment, pediatricians and child psychiatrists try to evaluate a child's overall functioning. How integrated and coherent is her mental functioning—the ways in which she shows her needs for food, care, and affection? What is the balance between her loving and assertive natures; between her intellectual and emotional expression; between her ability to be independent and her need and ability to accept care? We like to see a certain wholeness and evenness of progress across all these areas. Ideally, a child should be at about the same level in language and thinking, in social relations, in self-esteem, and in motor skills. A child with this kind of evenness and integration seems, even at the age of twelve months, to have her own personality. Children with some areas of great precocity or

remarkable delay—an uneven or mixed profile of development—may be at more risk for emotional problems. Unusual patterns raise the question about what may be interfering with the process of integration. Children who are living in stressful conditions or have had long illnesses may sometimes show unusual patterns of development.

Since children differ enormously in their normal rate of development and in their development in individual areas, such as motor skills and emotional independence, standard tables of development are only rough guides. Nevertheless, all parents compare their children with other boys and girls in the sandbox, the playgroup, and day care. If one child is falling noticeably behind in one or more areas, the parents' worry and your own concern are natural, and the caregivers should speak to their pediatrician. You may also recommend that they consult a child psychiatrist or psychologist skilled in conducting developmental assessments.

Charting Development and Pinpointing Difficulties

A healthy baby is born ready to become quiet when comforted, to search the world with his eyes and ears, to enjoy a good feeding, to make his needs known through lusty crying, and to show his contentment with sweet smiles. These inborn, biologically based behavioral capacities prepare the child to learn and relate socially. When all the innate systems are functioning well, a baby is quickly able to establish a special rapport with his parents and to regulate his sleep, appetite, and arousal. The care his parents give him, along with his other early experiences, quickly shape these core competencies.

Some basic skills that appear to be inborn actually reflect the interplay between a child's biological preparedness and a nurturing environment. For example, children are born with the mental apparatus to scan objects visually and to pick out certain shapes, but they learn what is important to pay attention to, and develop more sustained attention skills, as their parents engage them by talking, looking at things, and sharing one another's focus of attention. Babies who do not experience such quiet and sustained play and interaction may later seem to have an inborn problem with attention— even a disorder, such as attention deficit hyperactivity disorder (ADHD).

Similarly, children are born ready to babble and to communicate, but they learn to be fluent, creative speakers, with good vocabularies and expressive skills, first by hearing a lot of language around them and then by being engaged in communication by their families. The poor speech of an infant who spends hours in front of the television, and is rarely engaged in long baby-talk conversation, may seem to have biological causes. (See Chapter 5.) But children are born prewired to learn, and what and how they learn depends, to a great degree, on the intimate social world into which they are born.

Each child has a distinctive character, even from the first weeks of life. Some babies are angelic, while others are annoyingly assertive. Some take to nursing without thinking, and others need days or even a week or two to get the knack of breast or nipple. Some of these individual temperamental styles remain with a child over months and years; they become his personality. Yet a baby's temperament also changes with development. A calm baby may become irritable as he faces a new challenge and feels frustrated. He may settle down once his new skills, such as toilet training or eating on his own, are well established. The aspects of a child's personality that become reinforced depend on how her behavior elicits affection or annoyance in her parents. If you enjoy activity and energy, a quiet baby may be too boring, but if you are a quiet, contemplative parent who enjoys orderliness and calm, a high-strung child may prove an overwhelming ordeal. As a child perceives his behavior being reciprocated or rebuffed, he adapts it accordingly. A mismatch between the styles of parent and baby—where one persistently rebuffs the other—can seriously confuse the baby and give rise to emotional and behavioral problems.

Lines of Development

During the first years of a child's life, parents can chart the unfolding of her competencies along normal lines of development. These include the pathways from being fed to feeding herself; from being bathed to washing herself; from babbling to speaking in phrases and sentences; from biting to controlling her anger; from urinating and defecating spontaneously to being able to hold back long enough to use the toilet like an adult. Emotionally, a healthy child journeys from needing approval all the time to feeling inner pride in her own achievements. She moves from acting to please her parents, to doing things right because she does not like to feel ashamed, and to doing the right thing because she has developed standards of her own and wants to avoid feeling guilty for not performing up to them.

At each phase, children confront developmental challenges. These arise both from within as part of the push of maturation and from the world outside through interaction with parents and other caregivers. In the first months of life, a child's developmental tasks involve regulating her basic physical needs—eating, defecating, sleeping—and synchronizing her patterns and rhythms with those of her parents. The child who handles these demands feels secure and comfortable most of the time, and enjoys being held, soothed, played with, and fed. At age two, his challenges involve navigating the world more on his own, out of Mom's arms and Dad's sight. These tasks may be more demanding when the child is also with you in a childcare setting. Then he needs to modify his needs for the sake of the other children; to deal with their stimulation, aggression, and intrusions; and to adjust to the changing style of his caregivers.

A toddler's tasks in emotional development may include using her new, possibly scary, imaginative skills to deal with the birth of a sibling; being assertive enough to get what she needs without becoming a danger to others; and taking pride in her body and her gender. The emotional tasks that come with childhood and adolescence center around a child's increasing responsibilities, autonomy, and styles for expressing and satisfying needs (hunger, care for his own body, affection), showing and accepting love, and dealing with his own anger and the anger of others.

With maturation, there is increasing harmony between ambitions, abilities, and values.

Development along these pathways continues throughout life. A child may wish for the impossible—to become as strong as Dad or as rich as a star baseball player—with little regard for the realities of time, power, hard work, and the rights of others. As a child gets older, his ambitions, abilities, and values start to balance out, and he will learn to wish and to work for things that are within reach and consistent with his sense of right and wrong.

The aspect of a child's social development that starts at age two, when she moves from playing on her own to having fun when other children are playing nearby, evolves into the pleasure of having a best friend at age eleven and then the satisfaction of intimate partnership in young adulthood. For navigating through society, children move from primary dependence on parents, to reliance on peers, and then to reliance on their own personal skills.

When Development Does Not Seem Normal

All children go through slow or difficult periods, even occasionally regress. Nevertheless, a child who exhibits a symptom of mental distress or physical impairment can worry parents and grandparents—and other caring adults, like you. Is this a normal symptom like the occasional squeak a fine piece of equipment gives off? Or is it a sign that something is seriously awry? One way of assessing a child's symptoms is to consider the tasks he is facing, how stressful these are, and how well he is coping with the anxiety that is part of that challenge.

Toddlers typically say a loud "No!" to almost any request, but should preschoolers do the same? If children vary in their development and learn physical skills at different ages and different levels of proficiency, when should you be concerned about, say, a child's clumsiness? Patterns of normal development provide a framework for answering such questions. A child's variations from those so-called normal patterns can be especially useful in evaluating mental health, where trouble is often less obvious than a physical problem might be. (See Chapter 10.)

When assessing a child who seems troubled, professionals consider his strengths as well as his difficulties. He may be having a terrible problem in one area—with his temper, for example—but is he doing well in other ways? Most importantly, how is his overall adaptation? Aside from his problematic temper, is he moving ahead in his social skills or communication or self-care? Only when a problem interferes with the forward momentum of development does it become a concern for clinical evaluation and help. A child's symptoms are especially worrisome when something seems to be impeding integration and harmony; when progress is especially uneven or delayed; or when he is falling behind in adapting to life at home, in school, and in the community. Clinical understanding of a child focuses not only on a single behavior or symptom—such as slowness to walk, overactivity, or a tic—but on the full picture of the child as a whole person.

Children who successfully meet the goals of emotional development can love wholeheartedly and work hard. They take pride in their achievements, enjoy the feeling of progress, and accept disappointments and losses without becoming sour. They fight fair and shake hands at the end of a battle. When they fall off the horse, they get right back on or decide to try a different challenge. None of this is easy. Each task of development helps a child acquire new emotional, intellectual, and motor skills. At the same time, each can overchallenge a particular child and become a nodal point for emotional and behavioral problems. By thinking about any child's developmental situation—the challenges that he unconsciously and consciously experiences at a particular moment in his particular family—you may get a clue about the emergence of a particular symptom or problem.

Successful Development

If all goes well in pregnancy, human babies come into the world biologically ready for many environments—hence the wide range of cultures and family structures with which our species has populated and developed the globe's continents. With every child growing and developing at his or her own pace, siblings may develop very differently from one another: one may talk early, while another is slow to use even single words. Children may respond quite differently to the same parenting styles. Whatever their individual differences may be, aim to provide children with consistent, predictable care.

An infant's innate, all-purpose readiness quickly adapts to her particular world through the predictable and confident caring activities of her parents. When adults care for children, they do much more than just feed, or bathe, or comfort. They help the child's brain develop (see Chapter 2), shaping her temperament and personality (see Chapter 8), and teaching her how to function in the world.

A crying three-month-old turns toward the sound of her father's voice, quiets, looks intently, slowly smiles, and begins to coo. Her father can smile back and take this moment of alert attention to tell his baby a story about her grandfather, sing her a song, or just hold her close. In thousands of such moments of being held, fed, protected, and consoled, babies connect the sight, sounds, feeling, and warmth of their parents' presence with the experience of being distressed and then comforted, overwhelmed and then calmly attentive. Through these basic acts of caring, a baby forms emotional portraits of her caregivers that link experience and feeling and cause connections between brain regions to form and refine. These emotional portraits of protective, loving, listening caregivers to whom a child can always turn—at first, in reality and later, in memory and imagination.

These experiences in a child's first years—at home, in out-of-home child care, in the community—lay down the patterns for all future development. These experiences need not be painless and flawless. Indeed, they cannot be. But predictable, stable, nurturing care from parents, nannies, friends, daycare teachers, and relatives along with a baby's biological readiness to push her development forward and teach her to care for herself and, eventually for her own children. By being loved, stimulated, talked with, comforted, and attended to, children learn to enjoy the pleasure of being competent and successful and to tolerate disappointment and failure without sinking into despair. Such fortunate children will see the world as basically safe and secure. They will feel valued and effective, trust themselves and others, and be able to use their intellectual, social, emotional, and physical potential to its limits. This is successful development.

WRAP IT UP

Children were once considered to be small adults, until researchers in the late nineteenth and early twentieth centuries developed the idea of human development. They determined that a child's mental, motor, and emotional skills mature along a relatively predictable timeline. According to Piaget, cognitive development occurs in four stages. Preschool children are in the preoperational stage, during which they learn to work with symbols and language and begin to apply rules to their environment. Remember, however, that children do not follow the exact same developmental path at the exact same pace. Every child in your class will be different, but understanding the developmental stages leading up to preschool can help you meet your students where they are and foster their continued growth and development.

CHAPTER 2

The Developing Brain and Unfolding Mind

Understanding the brain and mind of the child who bounds in your preschool door begins with learning the complexities of brain development from the prenatal stages through early childhood.

A two-year-old looks across the backyard and sees the neighbor's puppy. "Dog! Me see dog!" he says gleefully. He glances up at his father, smiles, jumps off the bottom step of the porch, and runs across the yard. Just as he approaches the puppy, he slows down, looks at it carefully, and then looks back to his father, who nods encouragingly. The boy stoops to pet the puppy, laughs and giggles, and rolls on the ground with the puppy tumbling on top.

In this brief moment, thousands of cells in this child's brain have responded. Perception, language, intention, expressing wishes and emotions, jumping, running, interpreting social signals, gently touching, exploring: these are complex behaviors that require connections among many areas of the brain. But such complex linkages do not occur only in a two-year-old's brain. Thousands of brain cells also respond when a mother comforts her crying three-month-old or plays peekaboo with her nine-month-old. Some brain cells are actually turned on or activated by these experiences; at other times, connections between brain cells are strengthened, and new connections are formed. How do environment and experience shape the brain, and vice versa? How do events in the brain manifest in a person's behavior—child or adult?

The Brain's Building Blocks

A baby's nervous system develops in a series of genetically coded steps. This development starts in the womb, reaches critical phases in the first two to three years after a baby is born, and continues throughout life. Between the sixth and seventeenth weeks of pregnancy, a group of cells called progenitor cells begin to divide. Some of the cells from those divisions do not themselves divide but instead become neurons or glial cells. The timing of this process depends in part on the baby's genes and in part on signals from other developing cells.

During fetal development, each neuron is "born" with a precise identity and job to do. The chemicals that it will use to communicate have already been determined. A particular set of regulating genes cues these neurons not to divide again but to migrate to a predetermined location in the brain; the genes then turn off quickly so as not to send the same message to too many other cells. Neurons follow paths laid by specialized connecting cells called "guide" cells that only appear early in pregnancy to guide the neurons to their intended homes. Once in place, the neurons still need the final weeks of pregnancy to mature and connect with other neurons.

Various environmental experiences can harm the orderly development of the brain. Certain events, such as substance use or illness during pregnancy, can alter the appearance of the guide cells and the timing of the nerve cells' migration, preventing the neurons from reaching their intended destination. In severe cases, the fetus is unable to grow and the pregnancy ends in miscarriage.

The fetal brain creates about 200 billion neurons, roughly twice as many as a child will have at birth and far more than it actually needs to accomplish any given function. This safety margin reduces the impact of failed migrations. Nerve cells that do not make it to their programmed spot in the brain, or are damaged along the way, are genetically programmed to self-destruct. These cells are cleaned up and discarded throughout fetal development and through the first months of infancy.

Wiring the System: Connecting Neurons

Neurons communicate with one another in two ways: through the connecting cells, much like the wires of an electric circuit, and through neurotransmitters that carry instructions to various cells. The neurotransmitters are made very early in brain development. Before nerve cells are ever physically connected to one another, these messenger chemicals convey many messages. The surfaces of all cells in the brain (and throughout the body) contain receptors that are ready to read particular chemicals.

Of all the organs in the human body, only the brain is formed by creating more cells than will ultimately survive.

Once neurons reach their targeted homes in the developing fetal brain, they begin to make growth factors to establish connections among themselves and among the different regions of the brain, so that they rely on the physical connections as well as the neurotransmitters. The growth factors communicate with other neurons and encourage neighboring cells to link up in a group. Neurons that cannot respond to the growth factors will be eliminated. The neurons also develop extensions (called axons) to reach other neurons and the connecting cells. The axons and smaller branching fibers called dendrites make it easy for the mature neuron to connect to many other neurons. Axons hook up to the dendrites of other neurons; neurotransmitters facilitate the passage of messages across the many connections, even to distant parts of the brain and body. One neuron may be connected to over 15,000 other neurons in a complicated network of neural pathways.

Late pregnancy and the first two to three years of life see an exponential increase in the formation of neural connections, or *synapses*, in the brain. Many of the neurons in the newborn's brain are still not connected to the crucial networks of cells. The newborn's surroundings and the events she experiences help to determine where and how many connections are formed. The network of neurons thus quickly adapts to the particular environment in which the child is raised. For example, if a child grows up in a setting where adaptation depends on hunting, her experiences will enhance those brain connections that support specific

perceptual and physical skills. In contrast, when a child grows up in a crowded city, his experiences likely will enhance connections that filter excessive stimulation and enable him to attend and learn.

The most important elements in the child's environment are her parents, family members, teacher's, and other caring adults to whom she begins to form attachments. As a child interacts with her environment—taking in a parent's tone of voice or a new caregiver's face, processing and storing that information—signals race along neural pathways and may activate new connections and new pathways. Enhanced connectivity among neurons is crucial to efficient processing and storage of information. The connections and neural networks formed early in childhood stay with the child throughout life.

By the age of two, a toddler's brain is as active as that of an adult. The three-year-old's brain is superdense with connections and nearly two and a half times as active as that of a college-age adult.

The increased brain activity of very young children tells us that toddlers and preschoolers are genetically primed for learning and for taking in the world around them. Neural connections that are activated many times by repeated experiences tend to become permanent, but connections that are not used often or at all tend to be pruned away. As this process of elimination proceeds throughout childhood, the super-dense connectivity of the preschooler's brain is refined and remodeled into a more efficient network. A child's brain remains extremely active for the first decade and forms trillions of connections. During this period of intense activity, the brain produces far more synapses than it will eventually need. This high level of brain activity and the high density of synapses begin to decline only with puberty, when mature, refined networks of neural connections can afford to be less active because they can process signals more efficiently.

The pruning picks up pace in the second decade of life, though not at the same rate in every area of the brain. In those areas that control basic body processes such as breathing or heart rate, few changes in connectivity occur. But in the cerebral cortex where the basic rational actions of conscious life (thinking, planning, remembering) occur, connections are dramatically remodeled. At some moments, thirty to forty synapses may be eliminated every second—suggesting that in peak periods of development, the brain is responding quickly to conditions that promote or impede learning.

By the time a child reaches late adolescence, about half of the synapses in his brain have been eliminated. From this point on, the absolute number of connections will usually remain relatively constant throughout life, though in certain networks the density of connections may increase or decrease depending on use and activation. Throughout life, the brain continues to both build and eliminate connections among neurons.

Thinking efficiently depends on using only as much of your brain as you need to complete a task. Research on the electrochemical activity in different areas of the brain during different tasks demonstrates that adults' brain activity increases when they address difficult tasks. But if the task is familiar or easy, there is little or no detectable increase in brain activity, and thought comes easily. When there are efficient links among neurons and brain regions, signals travel easily, and processing information requires little increase in energy or activity.

The Timing of Development

Some basic environmental experiences are absolutely necessary for the brain to develop fully: that is, the brain needs to be stimulated at a particular time for specific interconnections between neurons and brain regions to form and mature.

Critical Periods

For some regions of the brain, if the essential stimulation does not take place during a particular time (called a critical period), that region's function

is lost and cannot be regained. For example, as a newborn begins to see, connections form between neurons in the area of his brain responsible for vision. His eyes do not really see yet; they simply transmit information to those neurons, which must make the necessary connections—that is, learn to process that stimulus into an image. After birth, if a baby's vision is impaired (such as by congenital cataracts), the area of his brain responsible for vision will never develop properly. The child will remain blind even if surgeons later remove the cataracts.

As a baby begins to recognize patterns such as familiar faces, new connections between neurons form. The connections not essential for the task at hand are pruned, while the most essential or efficient connections are made stronger, especially in those areas of the brain important for memory and for learning. Such remodeling and formation of new connections is necessary with each new skill. There are thousands of these moments in the first two to three years, as a child reaches developmental milestones such as crawling, holding a spoon, recognizing familiar relatives, and appreciating strangers.

The task of putting the brain together in the first years of life and adapting it to the baby's world is monumental. The critical periods form a plan for building a brain. The construction plan indicates that it is best, for example, for infants to see well before they tackle the task of recognizing faces and expressions. If certain brain functions or activities are not activated on time, the pruning process begins removing the unused cells. It is then significantly more difficult for the nervous system to construct what it needs for these functions later.

While alternative functions may develop, these are never quite the same as the original ability. For example, a child who is blind from birth often develops a heightened perception of sound or touch. This sensitivity helps orient the child and provide information about her surroundings, as vision would, but does not fully make up for the loss. They become prosthetics for an ability that the child cannot regain. As the pruning process slows down, such extensive prolonged remodeling does not occur in a child's later development or in the adult brain.

The Stimulus of Stimulation

In the most basic way, rich and stimulating environments increase the number of connections between neurons and regions of the brain, while impoverished environments reduce them. Either possibility can have an effect on later development, although other events and systems of support can mitigate these early environmental impacts.

The stimulation infants need includes not only learning but also all sorts of sensory experience and an emotional bond with her caregivers. A child's capacity to control her emotions hinges to a significant degree on neural networks shaped by her early experiences with important adults. A strong, consistent, loving relationship between parent and child is expressed in many psychological and behavioral ways, but also biologically in the development of the child's ability to withstand, and even learn from, the ordinary stresses of daily life.

Since pruning is meant to give the baby a brain best suited to the environment in which he finds himself in the first months and years of life, an enriched environment during infancy is of prime importance.

There is no single "right" way to provide properly stimulating environments for babies. Warm, consistent, responsive parenting can take many forms and be given by many individuals besides parents. There is likely a considerable safety margin between too much and too little stimulation for optimal brain development. Decreased stimulation resulting from a parent's illness or a change in caregivers will not crucially reduce the connections in the baby's developing brain. Further, there is a limit to how much stimulation babies can take in. Babies, like adults, need "down time" to process several hours' worth of experiences. Too much stimulation can overwhelm the baby, causing him to shut down for a time, unable to take much in, before seeking out more stimulation when he is ready to receive it.

The amount of stimulation a baby can tolerate will change as she grows. A three-month-old might feel overwhelmed by a loud family gathering because her brain is not mature enough to handle all the stimulation. In response, she might cry inconsolably or go to sleep. But that same gathering may not faze her twelve-month-old cousin, who has recently begun to walk. His brain has matured to the stage where he can absorb relatively complex information for longer periods of time with more people and more sources of stimulation. Thus, he has a more refined capacity to discriminate differences and familiarities in the people around him and can also, with his new mobility, seek out the people who seem more interesting, safe, or familiar. In essence, he is able to control, or ration, the stimulation in his environment.

Day-to-Day Help for a Child's Brain

Most families wonder about the best toys to provide for their children. They often want their children to have "the best" in order to make them "the best," but it helps to remind them that a single toy or set of toys cannot make a child mature or develop more quickly. Toys can help children learn and practice new skills, but getting the most out of these skills depends on the other, interconnected strands of development. Children can benefit from having access to toys that are developmentally appropriate rather than ahead of their skills. Furthermore, especially for infants, no toy can substitute for meaningful and stimulating interaction with parents or caregivers.

As teachers, optimize a child's brain development, work to develop a warm, caring relationship with him, expressing delight in who he is and helping him feel safe and secure. Each child is unique. From birth, children have different temperaments (see Chapter 8) and grow physically and mentally at different rates. Accept each child's own pace and individuality and hold on to the knowledge that every child can succeed in his own way. Learn to respond to the children's cues and clues and notice their rhythms and moods, and how these change throughout the day and over the week and month. Everyone can have good and bad days, weeks, and months, so try to understand what each child is feeling, what she is telling you in both words and actions, and what she is trying to do.

Preschool Development Tips

All of the functions we will discuss later in this book—including language, perception and motor abilities, and emotional understanding and control—depend on a healthy brain. The following tips provide a good base for areas of development in preschool-aged children.

- Take care of yourself mentally and physically—when you're not well, you're not available for the children you teach. Plus, the children worry about you just as you worry about them.

- Establish routines. Young children, who are still trying to figure out what they can and cannot count on, seek out familiar events and take enormous comfort in their presence. Create routines and rituals, and be as predictable as possible.

- Interact with the children. Play with them, following their lead. Children are good playwrights—they script, direct, cast, and act—so join their games. (See Chapter 4.)

- Talk, read, and sing with the children. Become the narrator of the day's activities. Surround the children with language and maintain ongoing conversations as much as possible. (For more discussion on language development, see Chapter 5.)

- Ask children what happens next in a story; get them involved in their own imagination. (See Chapter 6 for more advice about reading to children.) Play word games. Ask questions that need more than a yes or a no answer. Ask them to imagine what just has occurred in the past or will occur in the future.

- Talk to children about what they seem to be feeling. Teach them words for those feelings. (See Chapter 8.) When necessary, correct a child's behavior, but express that you understand his feelings. Explain the rules and consequences of misbehaving, and show him how his behavior affects others.

- Encourage safe exploration and play. Give children many opportunities to explore, to test things—and be prepared to step in if they are at risk of hurting themselves.

- Help the children explore relationships with others. Help them learn to negotiate with classmates and to solve inevitable conflicts while maintaining and strengthening friendships.

To help children get the most from the amazing brain they were born with, do all you can to nurture them—to enhance and broaden their experiences and help them develop a healthy curiosity about themselves and the world around them.

A Child's Unfolding Mind

Your *brain* is the physical organ composed of nerve cells and other matter in your skull. Your *mind* is the weightless, invisible product of that brain as it interacts with your body and the world. Your mind is your *experience*, how—consciously or unconsciously—you organize the signals that are continuously streaming into your brain and act in response to them. While your mind has no physical reality, in many ways it *is* your reality: through it, you receive a variety of data both from the outer world shared with others, and from the inner world of emotions, fantasies, and wishes that are uniquely yours. In your mind, you imagine ways to deal with those data and try to delve into the minds of other people. For you—or anyone—to be a fully functioning, comfortable human being, your mind must perform all these tasks.

As children's brains develop, so their minds unfold along three interwoven strands: physical, cognitive, and social-emotional. For example, a child's ability to ride a bicycle depends on mental skills that include her practiced sense of balance, her memory that persistence can pay off, and her capacity to interpret her parents' directions. In turn, a young bicyclist's ability to go farther and faster makes her think about her world in new ways. And, although we treat them separately, the

cognitive mind that learns, reasons, and makes choices is not really separate from the feeling and imagining mind. Feeling and imagining are central to how people behave, to what they do and say, and to how they learn and make decisions.

Emotions and imagination play roles in everything you do, starting with the way your mind translates all of your experiences into memories. Emotions color how you communicate with others; they fill in what words cannot express easily, if at all. You are constantly tending to the ways other people respond to you and express themselves. You can choose (or learn) not to act upon these observations; you can even ignore another person's feelings. Nevertheless, emotions remain a vital part of every interchange between two adults, between parents and children, between a child and his peers, and even in your solitary discussions with yourself. (See Chapter 8 for more on emotional development.)

The same is true for the mind's ability to imagine and fantasize. For example, parents often imagine their children long before they are born and view them through the mental picture of who they want them to become.

A feeling and imagining mind is the vehicle for all of these healthy, regular activities, and influences how you see and experience the world. Depending on a person's frame of mind, imagine how a sunset may seem brilliant in its play of colors or sad, even frightening if a parent is facing another lonely night with a sick baby. The mind shapes the meaning of each experience.

Social Interpretation

In every interaction, you observe other people's behavior and remarks and make judgments to try to determine what the other person is thinking. In doing so, you make assumptions about what is going on in someone else's mind. The closer you are to a person, the more assumptions you probably make. When a child goes to the toy shelf, you assume she wants to play. If the child curls up on the floor in the middle of the day, you assume she is tired or sick.

Often there are two or more possible explanations for a person's behavior. If a friend does not call when he said he would, you may worry that something has happened to him or resent that he does not care about your relationship. Which explanation do you act on? Which makes the deeper impression on your memory? Your frame of mind at the moment may influence your interpretation.

You do this kind of mental work every moment of the day. On the whole, despite the pitfall of assuming too much, you are usually accurate in your assessments. Your interpretation of what you can't see is informed by what you can. This evaluation happens in your imagining and feeling mind, informed by your thinking, cognitive mind. Social conventions have taught you to follow through on what you promise, so something must be wrong if a person violates these conventions. Experience tells you that children get a toy when they want to play. Experience tells you that a child who lies down in the middle of the day may have a fever.

Fortunately, your mind can also revise its initial assumptions when you gather further information. For example, when a new student joins your class and does not share a toy truck even though another student has politely asked him to do so, you might assume the boy is behaving badly, but what if you discover that the boy does not speak English? Your interpretation of the boy's behavior changes, and your own response shifts accordingly. Rather than intervene to give the other student a turn, you might show the student how to communicate her request with gestures instead of words.

Interpreting other people's thinking and feeling minds from their behavior and words is part of being human. Sometimes this mental process is interrupted by different conditions in the brain, which cause people to have difficulty interpreting other people's thinking. In some cases, those interferences can lead to autism spectrum disorder and other conditions. Social interpretation is therefore a developmental skill that a young child needs to achieve. Over time, he learns that many events go on in his mind— thinking, feeling, worrying, learning, remembering, wishing, dreaming— and that all of these are unique to him. He also learns that other people's behavior gives clues to what is going on in their minds. In imaginary play, children practice these "mind-behavior" questions: they practice the mental language of living in a social world that can be as confusing as it is comforting. Such rehearsals are an important step toward the adult's ability to participate in full and deep loving relationships with friends, partners, and even one's own children. (For more on play, see Chapter 4.)

A Child's Communication

A child develops an imagining and feeling mind through thousands of moments in the company of his parents. When a baby coos and smiles when his father rubs his head, he may say, "Tell me more." Parents pretend to have a conversation—adding meaning to coos, pausing at appropriate moments, even playing both roles in the dialogue. Their

Understanding Autism Spectrum Disorder

In 1943, Leo Kanner, a pioneer in child psychiatry, described a group of children who he thought had been born without a natural "attraction" to people, even their parents and siblings; instead, they preferred looking at and touching inanimate objects. Kanner called this condition "autism." These children's failure to interact with people disrupted many aspects of their development, including their language and communication skills, their play, and their imagination.

For about twenty-five years after Kanner's work was published, psychologists held the misguided belief that bad parenting caused autism. In the mid-1970s, scientific studies began to show that autism occurs in all societies and cultures and that it is a congenital disorder of the brain that may have a genetic component. Children with autism share profound deficits in social interaction, but the degree to which each child is affected differs. Children with autism also may exhibit profound disabilities in language and communication, and the severity of these difficulties varies as well. Due to the broad range of criteria for autism, it is now called "autism spectrum disorder" (ASD).

Children with ASD may also display repetitive and purposeless movements, ritualistic behaviors, difficulties with minor changes in the environment, unusual sensitivity (to light, sounds, or pain), and attachment to an object. Some injure themselves repeatedly.

About 70 percent to 80 percent of children with ASD also have intellectual impairment. Nevertheless, some are bright individuals who simply have profound social and communication impairments. A small minority of intellectually impaired children with ASD have so-called savant skills, which may include advanced abilities in drawing, music, calendar calculation (knowing the day of the week on which a given date falls), or memorizing trivial information.

Despite decades of research into ASD, no clear cause has ever been identified. Research implicates some areas of the brain involved in understanding social stimuli, such as the limbic system. There also seems to be a genetic factor, with incidences being higher in identical twins, siblings, and extended families. Because autism is one of the most researched disorders of childhood, and because of formidable advances in genetics and brain research, our understanding of the condition is likely to improve markedly in the coming years.

While there is no cure for ASD, many educational treatments can help children maximize the language and learning abilities they do have. In most cases, an autistic child needs intensive and structured schooling, often individually or in a small group. Research has shown that early and intense educational interventions may considerably alter the course of the disorder.

feeling and imagining minds are providing a foundation for emotional understanding. Though the baby is not yet able to join in the verbal play, he experiences his parents' pleasure, admiration, and responsiveness.

A child also experiences the way his parent or caregiver observes his gestures and attributes intention to them. In other words, he experiences how his mother "reads" his mind to infer what he wants to do or convey. Of course, this does not always happen perfectly. It might take several guesses before a mother realizes what her one-year-old means by "da" or "ba." Research shows that the more a parent or caregiver is able to consider what a child might be *thinking*, rather than reacting simply to what the child is *doing*, the more the parent conveys to him the importance of understanding other persons' minds. Similarly, parents and caregivers who are able to consider their children's feelings, beliefs, and even wishes produce children who are better at this same task when they get older and who feel more secure in their personal relationships with other children and adults.

Interpreting a child's true thoughts is not always straightforward: caregiver and child get to know each other intimately over time, just as spouses do. Consider a fifteen-month-old sitting at the dinner table, happily crinkling up a piece of red wrapping paper. Her father comments, "Isn't that shiny paper fun?" When he leaves the table for a moment to get something, the paper falls to the floor. When he returns, the baby starts to point urgently toward her red juice cup. In the instant when the father sees his daughter pointing, he has two choices. He can read from how she points to the cup that she wants juice. Or he can see that she is pointing to something red like the paper, so she wants him to bring the paper back. Either response conveys a message about trying to fulfill another person's desires.

Imagine that the father takes the cup into the kitchen for juice. At best, bringing back juice might distract the child from the lost paper, but only temporarily if juice is not what she was really thinking about before. If the father sees the shiny red paper on the floor and retrieves it, his daughter probably smiles and returns happily to crumpling the paper, having learned that her father can figure out what she wants. A single gesture can thus have many possible meanings, some obvious and some more connected to an individual moment between a parent and a child.

Over time, parents and caregivers usually grow to understand what a child's different gestures, sounds, and emotional displays mean. Throughout the day, young children experience the benefits of having their feelings understood by others. They learn that this is something people do for each other.

As a child moves into her second year, her ability to communicate a range of thoughts and feelings expands, but parents and caregivers still need to do some interpreting and filling in. An eighteen-month-old may look at a yellow flower, look back to her father to get his attention, and then look again at the flower, pointing, even saying "da" or "lello." That, too, is the early imagining and feeling mind in action. The toddler is curious about the flower, wants to interest her father as well, and, most importantly, wants to share this moment with him. She expects, from many earlier and similar moments, that her father will join in this experience. Maybe the father will kneel and look at the flower on her eye level or even add to the moment by asking her whether she can find other yellow flowers. Responses like these come from a parent's feeling and imagining mind.

This interaction may last no more than a minute or two. Still, many developmentally remarkable interactions are packed into this brief time. When a child looks at an object, looks to her father, points, and looks back at the object, this series of events is something child developmentalists call "joint attention." If her father adds to the moment by asking her to find other yellow flowers, pointing out the scent, or telling a story, he provides a "scaffold," or structure, for the child to add to. In this action, he conveys, "Yes, I know from your pointing that you're thinking about the yellow flower and you want me to be interested in it with you. I'll tell you what *I'm* thinking about that flower, tell you something about you and me together, and help you learn both about flowers and about our sharing experiences with each

Human Curiosity

Curiosity has a mixed reputation. Sayings like "Curiosity killed the cat" and "Some things are better left alone" discourage curiosity. Yet curiosity is what motivates a child or adult to keep learning about the world. Curiosity can help a person spot potential dangers and opportunities and find new solutions to old problems and mysteries.

Toddlers are innately curious. To them the whole world is a vast undiscovered continent to explore. Their new mobility brings more places and things within their reach; their new language skills open up another way of learning about their surroundings. They are full of questions about all they see, feel, hear, touch, and taste. Underneath the child's endless questions is a driving curiosity about her own body and the world around it.

Events and circumstances can, however, interfere with a young child's curiosity. (See also "The Child Who Cannot Play," page 59.) To explore the world, a child must first be capable of sustained attention. He must not be overly anxious and worried. A child who has experienced trauma or serious illness may be less curious. There is already too much in his day-to-day life that is stressful and frightening for him to consider other mysteries. When parents fight or are in the middle of divorce, some toddlers may show diminished curiosity. Likewise, school-age children and adolescents show the most curiosity when they are rested, relatively free of stress, and are given enough time for reflection and observation.

Encourage and nourish curiosity in young children by responding to their questions and by wondering aloud with them about things you see. As your inquiries encourage children to wonder with you and to observe their world, you demonstrate the value of asking questions and thinking about people and events beyond what you can see on the surface. Children who are more curious are able to use their intelligence more fully, can be more creative and flexible in their thinking and learning, and are more imaginative as older children and adults.

other." The father does not have to explain how this stimulates his child's imagining and feeling mind, and, indeed, a toddler will not understand it explicitly anyway. The lesson is contained in what her father does. The father also stimulates his child's own curiosity by showing her that he is interested in her mind and in her sharing her mental world with him.

Simple activities occurring every day are the stuff of learning: hanging up a coat, cleaning up toys, reading a book. At first, your mind supplies most of the action and content: you put words to the child's behavior. But she is joining in, too. When she turns to you and points to the flower, she is saying, "Let's explore and understand this world together."

Working Through Misinterpretations

Part of understanding another person's mind is realizing that sometimes you both make incorrect assumptions and act inappropriately because of them. For example, if you were walking down the street and saw a man stop, turn, and run into a coffee shop, you might well assume that the smells drifting out the door had caught his interest, especially if they had caught yours. But perhaps this man remembered that he had offered to buy the coffee for a meeting that day or he saw someone he knew in the window. With experience you come to realize that sometimes people make decisions based on incorrect or false beliefs.

Realizing that people sometimes act on incorrect beliefs or feelings is an important step in a young child's social development. With this understanding comes the knowledge that other people may not see the world quite as she does, and that individuals behave differently because of their different states of mind. This distinction is not easy for young children to make. Imagine a three-year-old watching her cousin Sam put his favorite chocolates in a kitchen drawer and leave the room. Then she watches as Sam's brother comes into the kitchen and moves the chocolates to the refrigerator. When Sam returns, where will he look for his chocolates? If you ask a three-year-old this question, they usually will point to the refrigerator, since they know the chocolates are there. They don't consider that Sam might have a false belief and look in the incorrect place for his chocolates.

Four- and five-year-olds begin to understand how other people's states of mind can differ from their own. They understand that Sam will look for his chocolates in the kitchen drawer where he last saw them. They realize that people can be led astray by incomplete knowledge, false beliefs, or misinterpretations. This discovery helps them to master many simple but essential transactions that are a casual part of social life. When a school-age child's Aunt Maria gives him a present that is appropriate for a younger child, he can understand that she has a false image of how grown-up he is but is still trying to show him love. Eventually, older children can imagine that one person can have different states of mind, and may have more than one reason for a particular behavior and thus try to reserve judgment until they learn more. Accepting the possibility of false belief is basic to a child's recognition of the individuality of different people's minds.

Another aspect of mental life that adults take for granted is being able to change your mind consciously. You believe things today that you once did not know or disagreed with. Knowing that you have changed your mind is essential to social relationships as well as to emotional and cognitive growth. But young children do not yet understand that concept. Thus, you can go to an ice cream store with a three-year-old after he has been asking for chocolate ice cream all day, and find that, once in the store, he orders strawberry. If you remind him that he told you he wanted chocolate, he may say with great certainty, "No, I always wanted strawberry!" He is not being stubborn or willful; he just does not grasp the notion of a changeable mind. He knows that he wants strawberry and believes that what is true *now* about his feelings, wishes, or memories always has been (and always will be) true.

By the time children enter kindergarten, they have begun to grasp the idea of changing one's mind, but not yet fully. You generally cannot actually talk to a child about what she once thought or wanted until she is around six or seven. This is also about the age that children can start to look back on when they were "babies," recognizing that they no longer think, act, or believe things the same way.

Let's Pretend: The Imagining Minds

Late in their second year, young children start using their imaginations to investigate behavior they see in others. One child's toy bear may join her at the lunch table and, shyly at first, nibble on toast with jam. Although the bear may become quite sticky in this game, letting a toy pretend to do a real behavior is an important step in the development of an imagining mind. Your response will depend on the rules of your classroom, but at home it will depend on the child's parents' tolerance for messes and sticky plush toys at the table. The child's mother may address the real situation, urging her daughter, "Finish your toast, and *then* you can play with Bear." Or she may join in the play briefly, wondering whether Bear prefers orange marmalade or strawberry jam.

Or, she may strike a middle ground, commenting, "It's nice to have Bear join us for breakfast, but girls eat first in this house." There are many variations on a theme, and rarely only one appropriate response.

The important thing about such a moment is how the child's actions demonstrate her imagining and feeling mind. The child is beginning to pretend, to act out behavior she is pretty sure is impossible. This is very early pretending, sustained for just a brief moment. Indeed, she is not always certain that the game truly is pretend. She may insist tearfully, "Bear *really* is hungry! Bear really *needs* to eat!" Not until she is about four will she be certain that all this is a game of pretending and even be able to joke with you about Bear being "really, really hungry." (See Chapter 4 for more discussion of imaginative play.)

The ability to pretend is itself a big achievement. It begins when a fourteen-month-old "drinks" from an empty cup and smiles, or puts on Daddy's glasses and laughs. It comes into full flower when a three-and-a-half-year-old walks through the house claiming to be a big huge dinosaur who needs egg salad sandwiches to take on a dinosaur picnic. Between these two stages are many steps that establish the foundation for imagining—for thinking about and playing with things that are not actually visible or present. Being able to pretend not only gives a child the capacity to experiment with different roles and experiences, it signals a big step in his mental development. With it, he gains the ability to let one thing stand for something else—what we call the ability to understand and create a "representation."

Representations are all around you. A photograph is a representation of a real person or place. You expect symbols to conform to what you know about the real things. You would be surprised, sometimes disappointed, when a photograph is distorted or faked. The ability to represent is a critical developmental step. It underpins all mental life.

One of the most important uses of representation is in systems that people share, such as spoken and written language. For everyone who speaks English, the word "mother," indicating one's own mother or mothers in general, brings to mind a whole group of qualities. Those qualities may belong to a particular mother (she smelled sweet, baked me cookies, had a lovely laugh or a quick temper) or to mothers in general (they take care of babies, are understanding, always make things better). When you talk, without even thinking, you depend on other people's ability to use a shared set of representations. They understand what you mean by your spoken words and references, as well as your gestures and tones and facial expressions.

Very young children acquire this mental ability in steps. The first step seems simple: understanding that everyone can use one thing to stand for another. A picture of a person stands for that person but is not alive. This is an important concept for children and, in the very beginning, a hard one. In their first year, infants are interested in pictures. A baby will find pictures of people especially captivating, but she does not clearly match a picture to a person. This ability does not emerge until the second year, and even then, toddlers are not always certain about the match between symbol and reality. They may wonder why they cannot eat a toy apple.

Gradually, children acquire the ability to hold more and more complex representations in their minds. They learn to use something other than a toy car, such as a block, to stand for a real car. Then they create stories and more elaborate pretend games, making a box into a spaceship and a bowl into a magic helmet. They recognize their own pretending as well as the pretend play of their friends. During their early preschool years, children begin to understand differences between mental and physical events. They start to appreciate that another person viewing an event from a different position may not see the same thing he sees. Very young children seem to believe that if they cover their eyes and cannot see a person, that person cannot see them either, but a preschooler knows that if she wants to hide from her brother under a blanket, she has to cover her whole body and lie still. Preschool children also begin to recognize that people feel happy or sad depending on whether they get what they want.

In their second and third year, children also begin to view people differently from objects. A child sees that other people are very like him. People move and act at will, and sometimes respond to his requests and communications, while even his favorite toys do not respond so promptly, though he can pretend they do. During this time, children also begin to develop a capacity for empathy. They recognize that a person is hurt or sad. They try to offer comfort or ask, "What's wrong?" They thus start to experience other people not just as doers but also as experiencers—as individuals who react to the world with feelings as well as actions.

Discovering Their Own Inner Worlds

By their fourth birthday, children make another significant step in mental development. A preschooler begins to fathom that other people have beliefs about the world around him that may be different from his own beliefs. Every person, therefore, has his or her own, unique thoughts. Four- and five-year-olds can understand that their thoughts, feelings, wishes, and beliefs are private unless they tell other people. At this age, children recognize that someone might believe something and might act on that belief even though another person knows it is wrong. Four- and five-year-olds begin to appreciate deception and illusion. They can play tricks, such as hiding or moving an object, knowing that people will look for it where they last knew it to be.

Throughout the school years, a child's understanding of what is going on in his thinking and imagining mind becomes more elaborate. He comprehends memory, concepts of time, and how thoughts and beliefs can change. He recognizes thinking as an activity people do to solve problems and understand one another. He knows that people think and imagine even when they are not pretending—that a person can create and enjoy a full imaginary life parallel to real life. These developments in a child's awareness of thinking, believing, wishing, imagining, and remembering are all part of her unfolding physical, cognitive, and social-emotional world and her own personal inner mental world. That world, unique to every child, forms the center of her individuality.

WRAP IT UP

The human brain begins as a few nerve cells early in fetal development and follows a remarkable path to a fully functioning brain as a child grows. Children's brains are extremely active and primed for learning. Their experiences can solidify some neural connections and allow others to be pruned away, making their brains efficient. Teachers can help with this brain development by establishing routines, interacting with their students, encouraging safe exploration and play, and helping children explore relationships. These actions can also help with physical, cognitive, and socioemotional development of children's minds. You can help your students learn to interpret others' actions and behavior and to process misunderstandings. You can help them understand how to use representations, such as with language or symbols. And perhaps most importantly, you can help them understand their individuality as they discover their personal inner mental worlds.

CHAPTER 3

How Children Develop Motor Skills

Motor skills are about movement, and so much more. Each time a child lifts a spoon, turns a page, or takes a step represents a leap and a connection between the brain and body.

Infants, toddlers, and preschoolers grow rapidly. As their bodies grow, they also learn how to move around and explore their world. Physical development in the early years of life is more than just learning to walk. It's also about a child's learning to feed himself, establish regular sleeping habits, master toileting, and become curious about his own body and gender.

There are two main divisions of motor development: gross and fine. Gross motor development is the child's mastery of the larger muscles of the body—those that control the major movements of the trunk and extremities. Fine motor development involves the muscles that control smaller and more pinpointed movements, particularly those of the hands and fingers. The earliest progress occurs in the gross motor realm.

While some aspects of physical development move along more or less on a timeline, parents play an important role in shaping their child's pleasure in his body and delight in his many new physical achievements. When they care for their child's body by bathing and dressing him, they help his physical development by reassuring him that they not only understand his rapidly growing and changing body but are not afraid of it. For very young children, their bodily skills are both exciting and frightening. Sometimes a child learns to walk before she is fully able to understand that her mother is in the room she just left. In this chapter, we discuss how children learn to control their bodies.

Gross Motor Skills

Children generally learn how to sit up, crawl, walk, and otherwise control their bodies in a regular sequence: that is, from head to toe or, in technical language, in a cephalocaudal direction. The order of these developments never changes, but the exact timing differs from child to child. There is a fairly broad range of normal variability, so you should not try to compare one child to another.

Newborn Motor Skills

The normal newborn infant has a limited repertoire of motor skills, of which a fair number are reflexive rather than voluntary. For example, she can turn her head but not lift it, and she can kick her feet and legs, but those limbs cannot support her weight. A newborn cannot support her weight against gravity.

There are two major reasons for these limitations. First, a newborn's muscles are immature. Like almost everything else in the newborn's body, the muscles and most of their attachments are formed and intact, but they are far from finished in terms of strength and function. The young infant's other major limitation is that the central nervous system does not have complete control of those muscles. Much of that system is not yet organized well enough to generate and transmit the commands needed to make the muscles perform in their adult fashion. The wiring is not fully formed. As nerves develop, they acquire a protective sheath called myelin, which functions somewhat like the insulation around electrical wires. Just as insulation allows electricians to create integrated but separate circuits, myelin improves the performance of nerves and smoothes the way they stimulate particular muscle groups. Furthermore, in a newborn's body, many of the nerves that grow out from the lower levels of the spinal canal have not even reached their destination in the muscles of the legs and the sphincters of elimination. Even if those muscles were in full adult shape, the infant would still not be able to walk or control his bowels or bladder. So the baby's gains in motor coordination reflect nerve growth and increasing nerve insulation through the myelin.

Much of a newborn baby's major activity is prompted by the startle response or reflex. This physical reaction usually fades after the first two months of life. Another easily seen newborn reflex is palmar grasping, when a child automatically grasps a finger. This response lasts until she is about six months old. These reflexes are a holdover from earlier evolutionary epochs in human development when parents needed an infant to grip automatically when they moved or sensed danger.

Newborns have other innate physical reflexes that have developed to help them obtain food. Even in the womb, a fetus is sucking, usually on her thumb. After birth, as soon as a nipple or baby bottle or anything similar touches the roof of her mouth, her sucking reflex kicks in. Also helpful for infants' feeding is the rooting reflex: when something strokes a newborn's cheek or lips, she turns toward that stimulation to locate a food source.

Other reflexes are less easily explained by the baby's needs. For instance, if you hold a one-month-old baby under the arms (supporting his head carefully) and dangle his feet on a firm surface, he will probably react by moving one leg in front of the other, as if trying to walk. These are not precocious first steps, since a newborn's leg muscles and coordination are not nearly powerful enough to walk, even with an adult's help. This stepping is a reflex and lasts only about two months. Later in the baby's first year, similar movements are voluntary and represent the real start of learning to walk. Indeed, after the first several weeks of life, almost all of a child's major motor activities—even seeking her mother's breast and sucking—are voluntary.

An infant's first intentional actions are holding up his head and keeping it from wobbling, and then lifting his head up from a prone position. After his facial muscles develop, he can smile. Next, he learns to control his arm muscles, so that he can reach for an object after fixing his gaze on it. He becomes able to move his extremities across the midline of the body; this allows him to reach with either hand and to

transfer objects from one hand to the other. At this point, it becomes possible to pull an infant from a supine to a sitting position while the muscles of her upper trunk provide some balance. Then, the child begins working on standing. Initially, an infant can support weight on her legs but can only provide rigid support. Before she walks, an infant recapitulates all these steps on her own rolling over, working into a sitting position, crawling to some piece of furniture, and using it for support as she pulls herself up onto her feet.

Steps to the First Steps: Crawling, Walking, and Other Voluntary Movements

By the end of her first three months, a baby has probably learned several basic, voluntary movements. When lying on her stomach, she can lift her head and push her chest off the surface, supporting the weight with her arms. When on her back, she can kick or straighten her legs. It takes another month or so before she is able to roll from her stomach to her back, or back to stomach. By about seven months, most babies can sit up unsupported and support their whole weight on their legs, though they are still far from balancing by themselves.

In the second half of their first year, infants master several new physical skills. Children vary in motor development not only in timing but also in the way they achieve certain skills. Crawling is a good example. Most children get up on their hands and knees and move them alternately, but some children will begin by pulling themselves with their arms alone and others will scoot. Sometimes children will skip crawling altogether and move directly to taking steps. These are all normal variants and all lead to the next steps of major motor progress.

Crawling is exciting for a child, since it opens up much more of the world to explore. A baby of this age is becoming more independent. She learns to pull herself up to her feet using furniture or an object and move while supporting herself. At one year, most babies can stand briefly and walk two or three steps without help; others have begun walking. The timing of this achievement varies according to a child's interests, environment, and sense of encouragement. An important landmark in motor development, unaided walking also marks a watershed in the relationship between parents and child. As an infant becomes a more confident walker, he becomes physically independent of his parents. He can go where he wishes on his own. He revels in his newfound freedom but is still psychologically dependent enough to react with fear if he suddenly finds himself out of his parents' sight. For parents, the baby's first step is a foreboding of all the stages of separation and liberation yet to come.

As with so many other aspects of a child's development, the speed and ease with which she acquires motor skills depends on her genes, her overall health, and her interaction with parents and other caregivers. Crucial to mastering this skill is the motivation parents provide by responding happily and excitedly at each of the stages leading to it.

Learning to walk opens up a much bigger world for children: they can move farther, reach higher, and escape faster. However, there are still some important skills that a one-year-old cannot master. Her spirit of adventure may be stronger than her ability to foresee dangers, and she still needs careful supervision.

By the age of two, most children have passed through the stages of walking (or toddling) easily, walking while first dragging and then carrying their toys, running, and balancing on tiptoe. They can probably even kick something big and not too heavy out of their way. Many challenges remain, however: getting up onto chairs and sofas without help, walking up and down stairs, and bending over consistently without tumbling over. The coming year is the time when most children learn to jump, climb, and pedal a tricycle. Mobility remains a great motivation for learning new skills.

At four, the average child can both hop and balance for a few seconds on one foot. She can move backward and forward easily. On the playground, she can kick a stationary ball straight and throw a smaller ball overhand as well as underhand. Nevertheless, she is still a long way from being ready to play the outfield: she probably has trouble catching a ball and must wait for it to bounce first. Already mobile, the child's prime motives for learning new activities are independence and play. Knowing how to hop, skip, and jump, a five-year-old will turn his attention to mastering the swing set, the seesaw, and all the different ways to hang from the jungle gym. By that age, a child should be able to dress and undress on his own, use silverware (starting with spoon and fork), and go to the bathroom by himself most of the time, though for social reasons, he may ask his parent or caregiver to accompany him.

To a large extent, walking is the last major milestone of gross motor development. Children continue to refine those skills as they learn to run and jump, hop and skip, climb, ride a bicycle, throw and kick a ball, and attempt activities like gymnastics or juggling and do much more. These are important new achievements, but their significance pales next to that original moment of walking itself. From that time on, much of the baby's progress occurs in fine motor development.

Gross Motor Skill Milestones

There is some variety in when children reach the milestones of gross motor skill development and in what order they achieve them. Achieving them in a different order or at a different age does not necessarily mean there is a concern for a developmental delay. Here are some of the milestones as the Centers for Disease Control and Prevention identifies them.

Age	Gross Motor Skills
Two months	Lifts head up, push chest up when lying on stomach
Four months	Holds head unsupported, may roll from front to back
Six months	Rolls from front to back or back to front, sits without support, supports weight on legs, rocks back and forth on hands and knees
Nine months	Gets into sitting position, stands while holding on, pulls to stand, crawls
One year	Walks holding on to furniture, may take a few unassisted steps, may stand without support
Eighteen months	Walks alone, may walk up steps, may run, can use push or pull toys while walking
Two years	Stands on tiptoe, kicks a ball, runs, goes up and down stairs, climbs onto and off furniture
Three years	Climbs, pedals a tricycle, walks up and down stairs with one foot on each step
Four years	Hops, balances on one foot for 2 seconds, catches a ball after a bounce
Five years	Balances on one foot for at least 10 seconds, skips, does somersaults

Fine Motor Skills

The sequence and rate of fine motor skill acquisition varies due to temperament, how each child's environment motivates and rewards the attainment of certain skills, and genetic factors. A baby still being breast-fed will not be as interested in learning to use a spoon as one who sees that *spoon* as the key to all his food. A child who never watches her family members writing or drawing will not associate using a crayon and pencil with pleasure. And a child will learn to write letters, even rudimentary ones, if he has been exposed to letters and the stories they tell through

Children acquire fine motor skills in a generally predictable sequence but vary in how quickly they proceed from one skill to the next.

sharing books with parents. (See Chapter 8 for more benefits of reading with your children.) It is not always possible to accelerate a child's fine motor skills with a stimulating environment, because a little body needs first to become physically capable of each task.

As noted earlier, fine motor skills reflexively grasp an object pressed on her palms. If the object is a rattle or bell that makes a noise, she can shake it with pleasure. She can also bring her hands to her mouth, obviously a preparation for feeding herself. Until about four months, a newborn can swipe at an object but not seize it. By the age of six months, an infant can usually reach for an object with the nearest hand rather than with both. Once he has the item in his grasp, he can move it from one hand to the other. When gathering an object, however, he must still rake it toward his body. Soon this grasp gives way to a pincerlike movement of thumb and forefinger. Eventually the baby's whole hand becomes more supple and its movements more intricate and delicate, and he grasps things with all his fingers.

Normal motor development assumes two important factors: a child with an intact neuromuscular apparatus and an environment that facilitates each of his steps along the way.

As motor development progresses, an infant is, of course, becoming more and more skilled in other areas, such as language development and social interactions. The developments in all these areas blend into each other, allowing her to accomplish more complex, interwoven activities. An infant develops the ability to feed himself because of his increasing comfort with eating, his familiarity with a greater variety of food, and his desire to please his caregiver, as well as because of his increasing skill in manipulating his hands and fingers.

At twelve months, a typical baby is not only getting up onto her feet but finding new uses for her hands. She can poke or point with her index fingers, lift things by grasping them between finger and thumb, and let go of objects voluntarily. A one-year-old enjoys banging blocks and other things together, and moving items in and out of containers one by one. He may also try to mimic writing with a crayon or pencil on paper, but this is normal imitative play rather than a real attempt to communicate through letters.

In their second year, children start to enjoy creating things with their hands: they scribble, pound on clay, and build towers of blocks. They can fit round shapes into round holes and enjoy forming patterns. Most toddlers need more months of practice, however, to put other shapes—squares, triangles, and so on—into matching holes; this challenge requires not simply identifying the proper hole but orienting the shape to fit through it. At this age, a child may begin to favor one hand over the other for tasks that require particular deftness. Just over ten percent of children will write

more easily with the left hand, and it is useful to recognize left-handedness early so a child does not lose time trying to match the dominant style. Left-handed writers do not necessarily perform all other tasks with the left hand, but if you observe a child using his left hand to throw, eat, hammer, cut with scissors, work hand puppets, and turn keys or knobs or lids, the odds are that he will be a lefty when writing and drawing as well.

Encouraged by her parents and caregivers and by her previous accomplishments, a three-year-old can demonstrate many fine motor skills. She can usually turn the pages of a book, grasping only one leaf at a time. She can unscrew lids on jars, though screwing them back on properly is still a challenge. She can also turn doorknobs, dead-bolt locks, and other latches that are familiar and within reach. At this age, an average preschooler is ready to hold a crayon in the position for writing, as opposed to holding it in a fist, and can make lines that go more or less where he wants them. After another year, a child can draw circles and squares and accurately copy squares that you draw, but copying triangles and other shapes may take another year. An average four-year-old can also draw very simple people and copy big letters—if you show her how. Within another year, she should be drawing people and writing letters that you can recognize. She learns to handle tools like scissors and to brush her teeth and hair. By the time a child turns five years old, she has probably mastered all the motor control and skills that she needs to enter school.

Encouraging a Child's Motor Development

Obviously, certain inherited or acquired injuries or paralyses can interfere with certain stages of development. A child with cerebral palsy, for example, may have difficulty learning to walk and need help to learn alternative ways to get around safely. In some cases, serious diseases can set back or delay parts of the developmental profile, especially if they occur at critical moments when the child is making incremental progress. For example, after getting sick, children who have only recently become toilet trained may revert to wetting or soiling for a time. Fortunately, patience and specific remedial help by parents and caregivers, under the supervision of qualified physical or occupational therapists, can often go a long way toward overcoming these setbacks.

The basic requirements for enhancing a child's motor development are these: safeguard the environment, provide appropriate materials with which the child can develop new skills, and ensure suitable places in which to use them.

To enhance a child's development, do not just respond to new motor skills, but actively stimulate them. Provide age- and level-appropriate playthings and opportunities for children to develop skills and competence. Materials that children can manipulate and experiment with are essential.

Once again, we emphasize that every child is different. There are no strict deadlines by which a child has to display certain skills. Every child develops in his or her own way, and a preschooler who is a few months behind the average in throwing a ball or matching shapes to holes may be ahead in other areas. The pleasure a child takes in each type of activity depends in large part on the pleasure he sees in your responses. Help the children to learn about these materials by demonstrating their use, and let them know how pleased you are with their achievements.

WRAP IT UP

There are two major divisions of children's motor development: gross and fine. As with so many other aspects of a child's development, the speed and ease with which a child acquires motor skills depends on a child's genes, overall health, and interaction with parents and other caregivers. Crucial to mastering this skill is the motivation that parents provide by responding happily and excitedly at each of the stages leading to it.

There is some variety in which children reach the milestones of gross motor skills development and in what order they achieve them. Achieving them in a different order or at a different age does not necessarily mean there is a concern for a developmental delay.

Children acquire fine motor skills in a generally predictable sequence but vary in how quickly they proceed from one skill to the next. The sequence and rate of fine motor skill acquisition varies due to temperament, how each child's environment motivates and rewards the attainment of certain skills, and genetic factors. A child will learn to write letters, even rudimentary ones, if he has been exposed to letters and the stories they tell through sharing books with parents. It is not always possible to accelerate a child's fine motor skills with a stimulating environment, because a little body needs first to become physically capable of each task.

Once again, we emphasize that every child is different. There are no strict guidelines by which a child has to display certain skills. Every child develops in his or her own way, and a preschooler who is a few months behind the average in throwing a ball or matching shapes to holes may be ahead in other areas. The pleasure a child takes in each activity depends in large part in the pleasure he sees in your responses. Help the children to learn about these materials by demonstrating their use, and let them know how pleased you are with their achievements.

CHAPTER 4

Child's Play: Child's Work

The time children spend in their imaginations creating games and worlds to play in helps them make sense of the real world.

Healthy child development is closely linked to a full, vigorous imagination and imaginative play. This perspective has not always been accepted. Not so long ago, fantasy was discouraged, imaginary play and even fairy tales were thought to be harmful, and having an imaginary friend was considered a serious sign that a child had a poor sense of reality. Daydreaming took up too much time, allowing a child to ignore the practicalities and realities of life. Children who daydream, experts said, must be unhappy and unable to accept themselves and their life's circumstances. Up to the early 20th century, this thinking was even used to justify putting children to work. Even today, these old admonitions

At Play: Two Case-Studies

Six-year-old Douglas's glasses and quiet demeanor make him look serious and studious, old beyond his years. But when he sits down with his collection of plastic dinosaurs and building blocks, it's as if Indiana Jones has come to life. Douglas is both playwright and actor in a drama that spans centuries, defies gravity and natural history, and earns the admiration of his parents and teachers. So vivid and carefully crafted is his play that everyone wonders whether Douglas is headed toward a career as a writer.

Janice, on the other hand, seems to have great trouble playing. When the children in her preschool invite her to join them on the "fire truck" (actually the big couch) or to dress up like their teachers, this five-year-old shakes her head and sits by herself, clutching her favorite stuffed lamb. Her teachers become concerned. Janice is well developed in many areas: she speaks well and even reads one or two simple books on her own. But her discomfort with the imaginary games that engross her classmates hints at trouble. Indeed, the teachers know that Janice's family is going through great trauma: her mother is in treatment for cancer, and when the little girl's father picks her up each day, he always seems frazzled and depressed. Perhaps, with that sort of confusion at home, Janice does not feel safe enough to throw herself into pretending. And yet her teachers think that imaginary play is just the sort of activity that might help her sort out what's going on at home.

about time wasted on idle play and dreaming still crop up in advice to parents and even in curriculums for young children. Nonetheless, it is now generally accepted that imagination and imaginary play are vital and should be nourished as the earliest expression of creative thinking and the practice ground for a child's emerging social and cognitive skills.

What Is Play?

As preschool teachers know, play includes many activities. There is the rough-and-tumble of children running, jumping, chasing, and wrestling with one another, which is universal across most cultures and even found in different species. The young of many animals engage in forms of play fighting, which seems particularly useful for teaching children and pups alike how to cooperate and interact with one another. There are verbal forms of play that are uniquely human, in which children play with sounds and words, even inventing their own language and rhymes. Manipulating and exploring toys and other objects (such as rocks, leaves, shells, worms) is another form of play in which, through trial and error—looking, feeling, tasting, listening—young children learn. Babies enjoy peekaboo, hide-and-seek, and dropping things off their high chairs onto the floor—all ways to explore how things seem to disappear and reappear.

Pretend play begins around age two, or just before children are able to let a real object stand for either another object or something imaginary. When your toddler begins to brush his toy lion's hair, it is the very beginning of his ability to pretend. He is using playing with a toy (a lion) using a real object (a brush) to represent what you do for him. When he starts to feed the lion with a spoon, smacking his lips loudly and blowing on the spoon to cool the soup, he is going one step further: he is representing imaginary food. And when he offers that food to another toy animal or an adult, the full ability to pretend is in flower.

Children's pretend play varies in quality, content, intensity, and degree of engagement with other children and adults. A child's developmental maturity determines the type of play she is capable of. Children under three often play alone with a toy or other object. They may roll a truck around, making realistic truck sounds, even providing appropriate warning beeps as they back up. But they make no special effort to invite others to join their play. Even if they allow a cherished adult to join them, they are not interested in other children's help. In "parallel play," which is also characteristic of children three years old and younger, two or more children play by themselves but close to each other. They may even use similar toys, such as a bucket and sand, but they are not playing with one another. If both children want the same bucket, it quickly becomes apparent that they have not yet learned to share and cooperate.

Children three to four years old begin to engage one another. They share toys, pass them back and forth, even talk about the same activity

and follow one another. Their play is still not completely cooperative, however. A preschooler who has no real companion nearby may create an imaginary friend as a playmate. (See page 142 for more about imaginary friends.) At around four years old, children begin to engage one another in games with a shared goal and story. They assign roles, direct action, even continue stories and games from day to day. This is the blossoming of play, both in its imaginative qualities and in the cooperation that children now manage almost without thinking about it. (See "Filling the Toy Shelves" below for more information on appropriate toys for a preschool classroom.)

Filling the Toy Shelves: What Is the Proper Toy?

The toy business is a billion-dollar industry, but a preschool does not have an unlimited budget. You may hear that certain toys are all the rage or somehow provide the "best" opportunity for learning. Sometimes you may be able to provide your students with the toy of the moment, but if you do, make sure to mix it in with more tried-and-true and diverse play materials.

Keep in mind this general principle: the more a toy encourages children to use their own imagination, the better (and, probably, the cheaper). Building blocks and construction sets are toys that let children build and create what they can imagine or see on the boxes. Crayons, markers, clay, and construction paper are also materials that encourage children to create imaginatively.

Respond enthusiastically to your students' play and creations, and stock your classroom with the types of playthings that most inspire them:

- Start with miniature or play versions of common objects like telephones, shopping carts, cash registers, stethoscopes, dining sets, plastic food, and so on. These do not need to be expensive, battery-powered devices that really work: the children's imaginations will be all the power they need. Most children like cars, trucks, and other vehicles, but in a classroom, you'll need to stick to the miniature ones they roll with their hands and not the ride-on ones.

- Supply some costumes. Hats are most exciting and easy to take on and off as roles change. Children also appreciate clothing that you or your students' families may donate, but make sure sleeves or hems are not too long so the children do not trip over them. Shoes and costume jewelry, the gaudier the better, are always useful for dress up.

- Find some raw materials, such as cardboard boxes, egg cartons, plastic containers, and pads of paper. Parents sometimes joke that children enjoy the box a toy comes in more than the toy itself, and often they do. Children turn boxes into everything from TV sets to playhouses as they enact the dramas of their day.

The capacity for "make believe" requires a mastery of symbolism—of letting one thing stand for another, just as a picture of a car stands for a real car. The ability to understand the meaning of a symbol is a critical part of human life and communication. You know that an octagonal red sign or a blinking red light means that you should stop your car and look for traffic before moving ahead. Hand gestures can communicate, "Follow me," "Look at that," "Good job," or "Stop immediately." When children begin to create symbols or representations, they can enter a more complex and layered world of social communication, where imaginative play flourishes.

A child learns to use symbols in several different levels, or stages. In the earliest, a baby picks up a spoon and touches it to the edge of a bowl. She thus shows she understands this object's use, even when she is not using it for that action. A later variant on this stage starts when a child "eats" from an empty spoon and looks with a smile to her father as she nibbles. Similarly, a toddler can act out sleep, closing his eyes for a few seconds before looking to see whether Daddy is watching. This is early evidence for game playing: these children are pretending in ways related to themselves. One toddler communicates through smiles and giggles that she knows (or is at least pretty sure) that her parents also know that there really isn't food on the spoon, while the other shows that he really isn't asleep. One action represents another. A preschooler who pretends to feed a doll, put it to bed, and read it a story shows that she is capable of a more complicated level of pretense. Parents and caregivers can encourage the development of this skill. They can join in reading the story, be sure the doll is tucked in, wonder whether it is having good dreams or will wake up and want a glass of water. By adding to the game, you can join your students in this new type of communication.

When children begin using one object to represent another, such as turning a cup into a spaceship or a stick into a toothbrush, their make-believe abilities have become even more sophisticated and open up more avenues for expression. Adults may want to correct a child, out of an impulse to engage with the objects in a more concrete and literal way, responding with things like, "Oh, that's a cup, but I guess it can be a spaceship," or, "Be careful with that stick! It might be dirty." Of course, you need to be sure children are safe during their pretend play. But if a child is capable of this level of pretending, she is probably clear about what the real object is and does not need to be reminded all the time. Talking about things as they are rather than as what they might be is a natural behavior for an adult, who has, in many ways, set aside the ability to imagine impossibilities in order to cope with day-to-day realities. But if you keep reminding children of the difference between real and pretend, they may stop their play, believing that the adults important to them do not approve of it. While returning to imaginary play may take some getting used to, enjoy the invitation. If you're able to, let yourself suspend your own reality and enter into the children's play.

Imaginary Play

This ability to let one thing stand for another, and to fashion whole scenes and stories as part of a game of make believe, is a part of the necessary cognitive foundation, or scaffolding, for a remarkable developmental phase. Between about three and seven years children can be master dramatists. They are completely engaged in their imaginary world and in playing out their thoughts, fears, wishes, and beliefs. In some ways, a five-year-old with a highly developed ability to play and pretend is like a reflective, introspective adult: where the adult puts thoughts and fantasies into words, the five-year-old puts them into play and action.

For those of us most concerned with how children feel and what goes on in their inner worlds, the capacity for imaginary play opens a window into how a child's mind is taking shape. What a child means in her play is more important than all the mental or cognitive feats that make play possible. It's like stock car racing: no matter how well-honed the engine of each car may be, the race goes to the driver who can visualize his car on the track, feel how it is performing, and imagine the possibilities for using that engine. A child's ability to represent, to pretend that a bottle is a boat or a spaceship, is the engine that drives her play. To make fullest use of the possibilities of play, she revs it up. The more she drives her imaginary car, the better she understands how far her imagination can take her.

In play, children practice development. In their imaginary games, they test out and master various developmental challenges. When children play school or waiter or doctor or try on their parents' professions for size, they are using play to understand these situations and experiences in much the same way as an adult might daydream about a new job, a new home, or a romantic relationship.

By repeatedly telling the story of a major change in their life, such as the birth of a new sibling or of some traumatic event, children adapt to and learn from those real-life experiences. In play, children can also try out solutions and options that would never be tolerated or even possible in their real home. They can return their new baby brother to the hospital or leave him for creatures to find. In these ways, they can both express their dismay at having to share their parents with a new

In giving children a venue for practicing new learning and social skills and an outlet for expressing worries, play is also a safe way for them to try to understand the world around them.

baby and play with their fantasies for solutions. In his play, the child does not only represent actual events in his life. He can tell a real story or, like any good fiction writer who uses scraps of his own experience to tell an imaginary story, weave bits and pieces of real events into whatever larger story makes sense to him at that moment.

Through their games, children try to figure out what happens when grown-ups go to work or where the dinosaurs went. Sometimes what is going on in a child's mind can totally surprise adults. (See "Fact or Fiction" below.)

Fact or Fiction

Five-year-old Victor is playing with a new student teacher at his preschool. Victor gets the teacher to join him in a game of cars and weight lifting. He tells the attentive adult about his special strength and bravery and invites the young man to admire how high he can lift a toy car. Victor says that his mother's Honda was badly hurt. He becomes sober for a moment and starts to ride the toy car back and forth with race-car sound effects. Over the next few minutes the student teacher hears the story of how Victor's mother was in a car accident: the car was hit; Victor's sister, Cassie, was in a car seat; Victor was in his booster seat. His mother was scratched a little, but Victor was very brave: he helped out, and everybody was all right except the badly damaged Honda. The teacher listens sympathetically, making the right statements about how scary all of this must have been, how brave Victor was. To all of this the boy nods seriously and whispers, "Yep." Soon he changes the subject back and invites his teacher to join in a spirited game of who can lift the blocks higher.

For all the world, Victor's play seems to tell a story of a dramatic and scary event— just the sort that a preschooler would work out in play. And just like an adult trying to

avoid thinking about something painful, Victor changes the subject when he approaches his limit of being able to think about it. When the student teacher next sees Victor's mother, he tells her how sorry he is to hear about her car accident. Victor's mother is puzzled: there was no car accident, nor does Victor have a sister. The entire story came from the little boy's imagination.

Victor was not intentionally lying or trying to fool his teacher. In fact, children of this age are still hazy about how and why people say false things. Rather, in their stories and dramatic play, preschoolers assume roles that are uppermost in mind at the moment. To a child this age, the line between reality and pretend is fluid enough to allow him to step into an event that is, for a time, real and lively. Possibly Victor heard another child talk about a car accident, or saw one on television or while driving with his parents. His story may serve as an effective way for him to proclaim his own bravery and strength as he tried to make sense of feelings of fear and powerlessness. He may have created this story to talk about other feelings he needed to think about in play, even how to deal with this young man who had come into his nursery school.

At some point in their early school years, children move away from acting out imaginary play and begin to tell stories as a way to express their fantasies. Their imagination does not fade, but they rely more on daydreams, structured imaginary games, and written narratives to express their innermost thoughts and feelings. It is as if once children understand the world of private thoughts and daydreams, they do not need to express so much through action. They're able to keep their thoughts to themselves and reflect on their fantasies and inner concerns. Every child's imagination remains active as she grows up, and the more imaginative preschoolers go on to be imaginative school-age and adolescent children. A vivid imagination in early childhood is often a hallmark of a creative adult.

Creativity

Creativity and imagination are not one and the same, though they share some common ground. Imagination is literally the process of forming images in one's mind, both familiar images to comfort yourself and new scenes and objects no one has seen before. Only the latter are usually considered creative.

Psychologists and social scientists have tried to define creativity. While there are many definitions, there is some consistency among them. Most agree that creativity involves forming new combinations out of familiar materials or ideas, combinations that provide a new way of seeing or of achieving a goal. These combinations may bring together diverse materials or ideas, such as applying an engineer's point of view to sculpting or computer programming to music. Sometimes the results are so significantly new and different as to change a field completely. For instance, when the psychologist Jean Piaget asked how children know what they know and tried to understand children's learning processes in and of themselves, he applied a philosopher's perspective to the study of child development. Before Piaget, psychologists simply accepted that because children's minds were immature, they did not see the world as adults did. Piaget's work made clear that, if one accepts a different way of thinking and viewing the world, children's "errors" are not errors at all. His novel perspective opened so many new lines of inquiry that it completely changed how teachers and child developmentalists view what children say and do. (For more on Piaget, see pages 6–7.)

Another characteristic of creativity is the ability to think flexibly and spot several potential solutions to a given problem. Creative thinkers see

many sides to a situation and employ divergent thinking (as opposed to convergent thinking, which aims for a single, correct solution).

In one of the tests for divergent thinking, children are asked to list as many uses as they can for a brick. Both the number and variety of responses matter, especially the ability to come up with less obvious answers. Besides suggesting bricks for building, for example, a child might say they can be used as paperweights, decorations, bug squashers, foot warmers, conversation pieces, anchors, gifts. There is a clear parallel to a child's flexibility in how he or she uses play materials: whether a cup is more than a cup but also a boat, a hat, a spaceship, a house, a cave, a hiding place, and so on. Although some children are naturally more flexible in their play than others, you can support and encourage a child's attempts at creative approaches to play materials by accepting and even being curious about the cardboard box that is a castle or the old stick that is a magic saber.

The Child Who Cannot Play

Pretend play is as necessary to healthy psychological development as learning reading and math, and it can help children to learn and to adapt socially. It is, therefore, significant when a child cannot or does not play. Autism spectrum disorder is one condition that may limit a child's use of play in making sense of the world (see page 30). There are also many other children who, although they have all the necessary cognitive scaffolding and mastery of representational or symbolic skills, still do not play imaginatively. Sometimes these children are overwhelmed by chaotic or stressful events in their lives.

To understand such a child, think of how you respond to times of extreme stress. You probably do not daydream much or at all; you may not even dream much at night. In order to play and dream, you need some space and time. When worries and stress are high, you (and your brain) automatically go into a vigilant mode, as if you were afraid and responding to danger. (For more on this response to fear, see Chapter 8.) This extreme alertness limits your ability to use imagination and daydreaming as ways of problem solving, managing emotions, and relaxing. The same is true for young children who cannot play: Their external reality crowds in on them mentally and emotionally, depriving them almost literally of the room to learn to read their own thoughts and feelings. Because their external lives are so rushed and stressed, their time to daydream, imagine, and reflect upon their mental world is foreshortened. Sometimes children who have anxious personalities are also unable to play well. The intense anxiety paralyzes them, preventing them from talking in their play or from shifting attention away from their worries. If you notice a child who is otherwise developing normally but is not able to play, you might recommend counseling to the child's parents or caregivers. Psychotherapy or some other intervention can help children better manage their worries, allowing them the mental space for imaginative play. (See Chapter 10 on children's mental health.)

While you provide the space, time, tools, and occasionally the companion or audience necessary for games, young children supply the imagination.

Allowing Space and Time for Child's Play

Adults should take the role of the producers, rather than the directors, of a child's imaginary drama. Directing a child's play denies her the full opportunity to choose the topics she will explore or the directions her stories will take. Instead, you should give her the freedom to direct the play so she can follow her natural bent.

Toddler's Play

The natural curiosity of toddlers turns them into scientists, explorers, inventors, engineers, and artists all at the same time. Space for toddlers to play does not have to be elaborate or full of toys. They do not even need a separate room, especially if they are still working on separating from their parents. (See Chapter 7.) But a toddler does need a space where he can be as messy as he wants to be. They can spend hours exploring everyday household items. Indeed, simple toys often go a long way with toddlers who are interested in patterns and enjoy sorting things by shape, color, size, and other attributes. Further, toddlers have a short attention span: they do not play the same game more than a few minutes at a time and can casually abandon what a moment ago entirely engrossed them.

At this age, playtime does not need to be educational. It is equally important for older toddlers (as well as preschoolers) to have the chance to play with toys that stimulate their imaginations. Even though a child of two does not have the language skills to create sophisticated stories, she may enjoy walking toy people through their daily life in a toy house. Her ability to invent new games means that even playing in a sandbox can be a mental workout as valuable as reviewing her numbers.

Since very young toddlers are just beginning to learn how to interact with more than one object at a time, they might need some help to move their play along in interesting and exciting ways. For example, showing her how toy cars can roll in and out of a box ("the garage") opens up the endlessly interesting game of in and out, filling and emptying.

The line between real and pretend is still hazy for toddlers, but as they grow, they come to distinguish between real people and animated objects, although they still enjoy pretending and want adults to play along. This discovery tends to coincide with the important realization that other people think and see things differently from the way they think and see them. (See Chapter 2.)

Two-year-olds may spend a fair amount of time on their own with their toys, but they also want to be sure their parents and caregivers are generally in visual range and definitely within earshot. From time to time, they will check in and even invite help and companionship. Very young children may also need physical help.

Another quality of older toddlers' play to keep in mind is that they do not easily share or cooperate. When they pedal around on their tricycles, they will not take turns. When two- to three-year-olds play in the sandbox, each should have his own bucket and a shovel. Gradually they will get better at playing together, starting in pairs and then small groups. (See Chapter 9 on friendships.)

The Imaginary Play of Preschoolers and Older Children

The space needs of preschool (three to four years) and early school-aged (five to six years) children are different from those of a toddler. After a child turns three, it is usually not necessary to show her how to play anymore. At any moment she may be riding a pretend horse or rolling a ball or being a mommy. Indeed, a preschooler can turn almost anything into a game, even cleaning up her blocks in time for snack. Older children can be by themselves more and do not need to check in quite as much with their parents or caregivers. While they may want you to admire their creation or their game, they spend longer periods playing either with other children or on their own.

Just as young children need space for their imaginary games, they also need time. Although the school day schedule likely includes a number of activities prescribed as part of a curriculum, it is important to ensure children have sufficient unstructured playtime. They need time just to play, learn to entertain themselves, and explore on their own, whether they are writing a short story or a poem, painting a picture, working on some other project, or just daydreaming.

A common time drain for young children is screen time, although this is not a common occurrence in a school setting. Some people worry that screen time stifles children's creativity by encouraging them to play in only one way, recreating the stories they see, but children often make up new stories for favorite characters or use the stories they see as inspiration for new games. You may be able to tell what shows the children watch at home based on the games they play in school.

Children like to play outdoors starting at about age three. Age-appropriate playground equipment is invaluable for preschool children. The equipment should be versatile enough to keep up with a child's physical and intellectual abilities. A jungle gym that offers several ways to play—a ladder, a slide, a pole, a hanging bar, and so on—will get more use than a simpler platform.

At age three, children begin to use art supplies to express themselves. One child may set out to draw his parents, though you

may not immediately recognize the squiggles. This interest and ability are due to a three-year-old's increased fine motor skills and his increased ability to imagine and plan. At this age, some children may still need to be taught certain basic skills: how to hold a crayon or thick pencil, how to cut paper with child's scissors, and how to paste one scrap onto another. The art the child actually produces should still be up to her.

In the year before kindergarten, children come to value patterns and rules enough to play simple board and card games. However, they do not like losing (not that anyone does) and cooperative games like Concentration, in which players have the shared goal of finding every pair of cards, are often more fun than competitive ones. When a child is ready to play against someone "for real," she will let you know. Do not assume that simply because a child is advanced enough to read the rules to a board game, she is also sophisticated enough to understand those rules and their strategic implications. Board games test many skills, so you can offer challenges for every developmental level by providing a variety of games in your classroom.

Preschoolers sometimes invite adults to join in their imaginary play in a particular role. Remember that a young child may still be sorting out how much you know and may assume that you know exactly how he wants you to play. If he hands you a cape or a hat, it is wise to ask,

"Who should I be?" or "What would you like me to do?" In this way, you encourage the child to direct you and to help you follow his lead by verbalizing the scene or story in his head. Imaginary play is not always a story in logical chapters: it may hop from scene to scene, without any plot, rising or falling action, or logical conclusion. A child may suddenly end a particular play sequence because it seemed too scary or worrisome at the time. Or she may simply have gotten bored with it. Follow her lead. Finally, remember that a child's play is not necessarily telling a true story about her life. A game about a mean teacher does not mean that she thinks you are mean; it may be her way of preparing herself for the scary jump to kindergarten or she may simply enjoy being in charge of other children.

If a child has an invisible friend or playmate, or projects distinct personalities onto his toys, he may enjoy having you play along with this game. How comfortable you feel may depend on what else is happening in the classroom, your willingness to join in, or any suspicion that he plans to blame this imaginary friend for things he did. It is best to view the invisible friend as another story the child is telling as he works through the mysteries of his life. Imaginary friends tend to disappear by early school age, as pretending wanes as the primary mode of play.

After they enter school, children may stop being actors and start being directors. Instead of dressing up as doctors, princesses, and space fighters, they tell their stories through little toy people and animals. Many school-age children spend most of their time manipulating "miniature worlds." These may take the form of little cars traveling between a racetrack and a garage, a fully furnished doll's house, a plastic street lined with tiny shops, or a space station complete with blinking lights and aliens. Children's growing awareness of gender roles may well influence the type of miniature world they choose, but whether the little people are labeled "dolls" or "action figures," the form and benefits of playing with them are much the same.

Perhaps we should apply the phrase "child's play" not to things easy or frivolous, but to the most difficult and challenging tasks humans engage in: solving problems of all kinds and honing and concentrating one's social and cognitive abilities.

Play is a child's work. In play, a child has an opportunity to think about and work through day-to-day dilemmas like leaving his parents to attend school or going to the doctor. Children who enjoy the mental and physical space and time to play imaginatively learn more quickly, are often more socially skilled, and are more likely to remain creative and curious for the rest of their lives.

Healthy child development is closely linked to a full, vigorous imagination and imaginative play. Preschool children three to four years old begin to engage one another in play. They share toys, pass them back and forth, even talk about the same activity and follow one another. Their play is still not completely cooperative, however. A preschooler who has no real companion nearby may create an imaginary friend as a playmate. At around four years old, children begin to engage one another in games with a shared goal and story. They assign roles, direct action, even continue stories and games from day to day. This is the blossoming of play, both in its imaginative qualities and in the cooperation that children now manage almost without thinking about it.

Imaginary play, the ability to let one thing stand for another, and to fashion whole scenes and stories as part of a game of make believe, is a part of the necessary cognitive foundation, or scaffolding, for a remarkable developmental phase. Between about three and seven years, children can be master dramatists. They are completely engaged in their imaginary world and in playing out their thoughts, fears, wishes, and beliefs.

Children who cannot play are sometimes overwhelmed by chaotic or stressful events in their lives. Sometimes children who have anxious personalities are also unable to play well. The intense anxiety paralyzes them, preventing them from talking in their play or from shifting attention away from their worries. Psychotherapy or some other intervention can help children better manage their worries, allowing them the mental space for imaginative play.

Children need unstructured time to just play. Play is a child's work. Children who enjoy the mental and physical space and time to play imaginatively learn more quickly, are often more socially skilled, and are more likely to remain creative and curious for the rest of their lives.

CHAPTER 5

First Words and Beyond: How Children Discover Language

Many stages of communication develop before a three-year-old begins preschool, and with parents' and caregivers' encouragement, the unintentional sounds a newborn makes turn into words that evolve into sentences over a few short years.

Consider two responses to a thirteen-month-old whose language development has reached the point that he says "da da da." In one scenario, the boy's mother seeks advice from a specialist, concerned that her son's speech isn't more complex. Since children are expected to speak their first words between the ages of nine and eighteen months, she's reassured that her son is within the normal range. In the other scenario, a father is excited at the thought that his son is trying to say "Daddy." In reality, the sound is likely to be meaningless vocal play. The difference between these scenarios is the emotion of the caregiver: the father's enthusiasm may encourage the baby's vocal play as he tries more sounds, while the mother's worry is less likely to do so. This is an example of how parents and caregivers influence a child's language development.

Communication is, by definition, a two-way process. What you say to a baby, how you listen, and how the baby sees you respond all influence language development. This process starts well before a child's first word. Nearly from birth, a child sends messages—in glances, in sounds, in facial expressions and behavior. Parents and caregivers usually sense this and make observations such as, "If she doesn't like something, boy, does she let us know it!" These observations are scientifically sound: many basic language skills seem to be rooted in innate capabilities.

As an infant's instinctive attempts at communication further his language development, he is assisted by his caregivers' attempts to stimulate his ability to communicate. Most parents are pleased when their child develops a facility with language. "I'm so glad Rebecca and I can finally talk!" a mother might say of her three-year-old. "My oldest said something really clever yesterday," a father might tell friends at work.

Parents and caregivers around the world speak to their infants in similar ways that stimulate more frequent and more sophisticated speech. As language and communication skills develop steadily in the first three to five years, they draw children and caregivers closer together, at least until adolescents begin to test their improved skills in argumentation. In this chapter, we will discuss the earliest communication through babies' sounds, the toddler's discovery of names and love for labeling the world, and the preschool child's construction of sentences and simple stories.

The First Year: Communication Without Speaking

Being able to attract an adult's attention, maintain a social relationship, and inspire affection helps an infant survive.

Even before infants start talking, they engage in a great deal of communication. They take in information about their environment and express, as best they can, their needs and pleasures. Far from being a blank slate on which adults chalk the rudiments of language, an infant acts to hold adults' attention and elicit positive responses. This makes evolutionary sense. Without this early stage of language development, babies would be merely helpless, noisy, and rather unproductive members of society.

A newborn's principal vocal behavior is crying. Crying is mostly involuntary, a response to some distress the child feels. Although effective at attracting attention, crying is limited in what it communicates. Parents, especially those who hear a lot of crying, may be unaware of the other ways their newborns are sending messages. Infants begin life with a natural desire to vocalize and communicate. Newborns seem to have a common set of behaviors that cue adults to interact with them. These behaviors are so widespread and appear so soon after birth that they seem to be innately programmed.

The Sound Foundation of Language

From the first days of life, infants prefer sounds in the same frequency range as human voices; and within that range, they prefer speech to other rhythmic and musical sounds. When a newborn hears a voice, he looks for its source, his face registers pleasure when he finds it, and he becomes quiet and still until the voice ceases. He does not do the same when he hears other sounds. A three-day-old infant can distinguish her own mother's voice from the voices of other women.

Newborns are also attracted to human faces. They will always choose to look at a face instead of any interesting but nonhuman object, and typically their own face registers pleasure at the sight of a human face. Conveniently, parents interpret this behavior as a sign of an infant's willingness to interact, and they provide more stimuli—talking, touching, and making faces in response—to keep up the "conversation." The newborn infant thus appears to be already biologically prepared for human communication and language.

Young babies pick up other cues necessary for spoken language. An infant as young as two months may take turns in vocal interactions with his mother, staying

quiet while she talks and making noise when she pauses. Around seven months, babies become attuned to the auditory cues that adults insert into sentences to tell listeners how phrases fit together, and prefer looking toward the voice of someone reading sentences with normal pauses rather than one using irregular phrasing.

Stimulating Language in Infants

Being naturally prepared to learn language is, of course, not the same thing as actually learning it. Children found in extreme situations, growing up without meaningful adult interaction, consistently develop little or no language ability, even after intense remedial training. On the other hand, children in a bilingual environment learn both languages at the same time, and do so much more easily than adults do and are less likely to speak either language with an accent. A child's early years thus seem to be a critical period for learning language, and early interaction with parents and caregivers is the seed of most communication skills.

The "conversation" between parents and their children starts early. As early as four weeks after birth, a wide-awake baby looks intently at an adult face and makes sounds, sometimes imitating her parents' intonation.

As the baby grows older, however, the human face holds less fascination. She will look at an adult when she wants to interact but then looks away when she feels tired or overstimulated. This reaction seems to push caregivers to change their behavior to try to keep her attention. They stretch their faces into exaggerated expressions, talk more, and vary the intonations of their voice more.

Infants develop intentions at about eight months. They can use gazes and pointing to communicate what they want. Between eight and ten months, although still communicating mostly through gestures and not words, an infant begins to realize that language is a wonderful way to fulfill her intentions. She may even develop her own symbolic vocabulary, waving her arms excitedly up and down to represent a favorite toy kangaroo, for example (and also imitating her parents' demonstration of how a kangaroo hops).

As a child develops these capabilities, caregivers often believe that an infant understands more than he really does. In many cases, it is the tone of voice or the nonverbal communication such as gazes and gestures that accompany the words, rather than the words themselves, that the infant understands.

As soon as an infant reveals an interest in communicating, caregivers start asking for more. They no longer interpret every sound or gesture as part of the conversation and instead provide the vocabulary or withhold a response until she expresses herself through words. Caregivers thus shape an infant's skills and desires into language.

At each stage in a young child's life, caregivers naturally seem to communicate in the way that best encourages new language skills.

The Second Year: Words and More Words

The second year is a remarkable time for a child's language development. His eagerly awaited first words foreshadow his grasping the idea that objects have names and that other people understand those names. He can ask for a "cracker" or "juice" just by using the name. His next step is to put words together into short phrases and sentences. Even the phrase "my bear" is the beginning of a sentence and a story. It says there is a toy called a bear, and that it belongs to him.

First Words

The average child says her first word and takes her first step around the time of her first birthday. A one-year-old's vocabulary is small: she may understand fifty words but speak only three. Those three words most likely refer to objects she plays with, such as "ball," and activities she regularly does, such as saying "bye-bye."

Over the course of their second year, infants expand their spoken vocabulary. This growth comes in fits and starts. The first fifty words accumulate slowly, and often children plateau around this point. They may even drop some of the words they have learned. Children's word acquisition is also channeled by the types of sounds they can already make. A child who knows "bat" will pick up "ball" more quickly than "glove". Children under two realize that their most powerful vocal communications are still nonverbal and may scream instead of trying to state their feelings.

By eighteen months, the average child uses between 50 and 150 words. A two-year-old uses about 300 words and understands up to 1,000. The words in a two-year-old's spoken vocabulary are more complex than his earlier utterances, and include words with two consonant sounds together and words of two or more syllables, as in "Grandma." Most of a toddler's new words are nouns and are usually things he can act on. Thus, since a two-year-old can take off his shoes but needs help with his shirt, he usually learns the word "shoe" first.

Only about 70 percent of a two-year-old's words sound correct by an adult standard, and they may attach their own meanings to words. For instance, she may call every four-legged animal a "cat," even cows or elephants. Two-year-olds often know the names of several colors but may not know which color is right. Such mistakes in the second year may be part of a strategy to feel out the meaning of a word: a child observes adults' reactions so he can refine his understanding.

Creating Sentences

The next process in a child's language development is the creation of sentences. At first, their messages are single words. These can be as meaningful as a sentence—"Up!" for "Please pick me up because I'm tired of walking"—but easier for little mouths to get out. The next stage in sentence forming, around eighteen months, is to string two or three words into telegraphic messages: "Want cookie," "More cookie," "Two cookie!" By the end of that second year, a child's sentences can be three or four words long, but still telegraphic: "Mommy ball" might have grown into "Mommy throw ball." Again, the child's meaning is clear even if grammatical elements are missing.

A typical toddler's sentences reflect her interests and limitations. Because two-year-old children do not have a real understanding of time, they rarely talk in terms of what will happen soon or what happened yesterday. Two-year-olds usually understand the concept of a question, but express one with a rising intonation—"Doggie mad?"—instead of shifting the words grammatically. They also know the word "no," but use it as an all-purpose negative: "No go bed," "Mommy no bye-bye."

Toddlers aged twelve to eighteen months talk about what is right in front of them, and rarely add information that an adult observer cannot perceive. They have a hard time carrying on a conversation past two or three exchanges, especially if they did not start the topic. By the age of two, however, children can provide new information. They start asking for the names of things, and they realize that different words can express the same idea: "I thirsty," "Want juice."

In vocabulary, toddlers probably understand three times as many words as they use. In sentence structure, the gap between comprehension and use is much narrower. A two-year-old's brain can process only so many sentence elements at a time, whether she is speaking or listening. Caregivers sometimes believe otherwise because children in their second year are good at picking up clues from context.

Adults respond to toddlers' new communication abilities by further modifying their own conversational style. Their sentences are still short and simple, but often more grammatical than their speech to other adults, in order to model proper grammar. Research shows that stimulating a dialogue with children is one of the most effective ways to help them develop their language skills.

While two-year-olds rely on parents to structure a conversation, they can manage their response more easily. They know that a pause, especially at the end of a phrase, indicates that it is their turn to speak. They can but do not always stick to a topic and are more capable of repeating or rewording a sentence if their listener did not understand the first time.

A two-year-old also learns to speak differently to different people. He might talk to babies in a high-pitched voice as adults do, and address his parents differently from other people. A child this age assumes that adults know everything; he has learned to distinguish his own mind from others. Thus, some of his remarks will not contain enough information for another person to understand. A two-year-old might hold up a sticker and tell a parent's friend, "I got this from Shirley," without explaining who Shirley is.

The Third Year: Building on Words

Researchers have found that English-speaking two-year-olds acquire grammatical building blocks in a fairly regular sequence. First, they grasp how to turn *walk* into *walking* to express something happening right now. They learn that adding the *s* or *z* sound to nouns can make them multiply *(books)* or possess other things *(Daddy's)*. Next come simple prepositions—*in* and *on*. English speakers start using articles—*a, an, the*—relatively late. (In contrast, children learning Spanish often master the equivalent *el, la, las,* and *las* early, perhaps because those Spanish articles stand out more in everyday speech.)

Two-year-olds acquire a larger vocabulary of words that connect or compare the things they see. They are likely to understand many spatial terms such as *in, through,* and *next to.* They understand some simple adjectives, usually starting with *big* and *little.* They nail down two or three colors. Most can ask questions beginning with *what* and *where,* and some know *who* and *how* as well. While one-year-olds use *no* as an all-purpose negative, toddlers learn how to use *can't* and *don't,* often before they use *can* and *do.* Two-year-olds are also likely to start using pronouns, especially to refer to themselves.

A growing vocabulary allows two-year-olds to produce more elaborate noun phrases. You may hear a toddler using words to modify nouns, as in "my hat" or "red hat." At three years old, children can even try two modifiers together: "my red hat." After age three, they learn to use these phrases within a sentence, usually at the end: "I put on my red hat." (They are less likely to use complex noun phrases at the start of a sentence: "My red hat is dirty.")

A similar process turns toddlers' verbs into more powerful communicators. Rather than simply using the simplest form of a verb, they use helping verbs. Three-year-olds learn the past tense of irregular verbs, such as *came, went,* and *saw.* When the past tense sounds more like the present tense, as in *wash* and *washed,* a young child is likely to miss hearing the difference. The use of future and past tenses reflects another discovery of the three-year-old: the passage of time.

It is rare for toddlers to ask someone to clarify a statement they do not understand. Instead, they interpret sentences that contain unfamiliar words or phrases by guessing at the most likely meaning. Thus, a two-year-old who does not know the word *beneath* will probably translate "Put the cup beneath the table" as "Put the cup *on* the table" because the latter action is more common.

Parents' interactive strategies develop along with their children's abilities. Both an eighteen-month-old and a two-year-old might exclaim,

"Girl dolly!" when they see another child's toy. The younger child's mother is likely to expand that brief utterance into a sentence: "Yes, that girl has a dolly." The mother of a two-year-old typically responds in a similar way but asks for a response: "Yes, that girl has a dolly. Is it bigger than your dolly?" Neither mother explicitly corrects her child's statement, but the second one implicitly asks for more. She models a back-and-forth conversation and cues her older child about what to say next.

What's The Magic Word?

One of the few aspects of language that parents explicitly teach their children is how to speak politely. They have many reasons to do so: etiquette skills help children navigate life. People like to be treated respectfully, and in American culture, teaching children manners is a parental responsibility, and a rude child reflects badly on the parents. But parents also learn to be realistic. A one-year-old's first word will not be *please*. It is important to adjust expectations of politeness according to what a child is capable of at different ages.

Even a toddler can pick up the fact that "Cookie please" is more likely to result in a cookie than "Gimme cookie!" Research has found that two-year-olds use *please* most when the person listening is bigger, unfamiliar, or holding something they want. Sometimes children at this age phrase their requests as statements, of need instead of desire: "I can't reach," "I'm tired." When asked to make their requests more politely, two-year-olds may just add the word *please* or put a little whine in their voices. They are trying, but still need guidance about what people expect of grown-up children.

Three- and four-year-olds move beyond the mere word of *please*. With more helping verbs at their command, they can express their wishes in a variety of ways: "Can I have a napkin?" "Would you open this for me?" Children this age realize that they may have to explain their requests: "Get the scissors.

I can't reach them." By age five, preschoolers can embed a request more subtly: "Those cookies you brought in for us for snack smell really good. You bring in the best snacks in the whole world!"

Despite your best efforts to reinforce the manners their parents are teaching them, there are ways most preschoolers will never be polite. They are not subtle about gaining your attention when you are focused on another task or person. Nor do they have many persuasive skills. They still see the world exclusively through their own eyes, and have trouble recognizing how someone else's interests could be affected by their own. Consider two siblings who want to stay up late to watch a rocket launch on television. Trying his hardest to be persuasive, the four-year-old says, "I need to see the rocket." A seven-year-old might present the same request by addressing what is important to her parents: "I have to do a science report next week, and maybe I'll write about the rocket."

You may think that seven-year-old's request is manipulative, and it is. But so is the four-year-old's statement, he is just less effective. The seven-year-old is more persuasive because she has made the leap to considering what other people value. The next task caregivers have in encouraging moral development is to help children understand that politeness involves more than saying the right thing when he wants something. (See Chapter 8.)

In their third year, children still often drop unstressed syllables from words ("nana" for *banana)* or substitute an easy consonant for a harder one ("doddie" for *doggie,* "sair" for *chair).* It takes time for them to learn how to run consonants together, as at the start of "play"; by age two, a child usually has a few such words in his vocabulary, but combining more consonants, as in "scrape," can take another year or two. Similarly, by age two, a child is probably only using a few multisyllabic words. The most common pronunciation difficulties involve the late-developing consonant sounds: *l, r, th,* and *s.*

Some children may not master these late-developing consonants until well into their fourth or fifth year. The child is probably aware of the proper way to say a word; his challenge is to find the right combination of moves in his mouth to make that sound. Avoid imitating a child's pronunciation; instead, pronounce the words correctly. Only about 5 percent of children enter school with a pronunciation problem, and when they do, it is usually confined to only one or two sounds.

In their third year, children learn the many different ways they can use language. They are no longer simply expressing immediate needs or trying to get a response from their parents. They are conveying new information, talking about the past, stating their intentions, and even pretending. (See also Chapter 4 on play.)

The Preschool Years: Discovering and Applying the Rules of Language

By the middle of her fourth year, a child can express herself much more like an adult. This is the time when a child begins to explore the rules of language—how to indicate more than one dog, show her ownership of a toy truck but not of a toy shovel, put two thoughts together, and convey that something is already past or an event is yet to come.

Preschoolers can pick up new words at an astonishing rate of nine per day.

Preschoolers' vocabularies are growing fast. They expect each new word to have a unique meaning. When preschoolers learn a synonym for a word they already know, they often try to assign a different meaning to it: "An automobile must be a big car," for instance.

During this stage, they learn words for expressing relationships in time, such as *before, after, since,* and *until*. They can ask questions with *why, how,* and *when* and answer such questions correctly, although it still helps them to see the person or the object a question concerns. Four-year-olds have added more adjectives to their vocabulary. With

pairs of adjectives, as in *thick* and *thin,* they usually first learn the word that denotes the larger measure. Preschoolers also start to use *more* and *less*, though at first they might mix these up, using both to mean "a different amount." By age five, children have mastered comparative and superlative adjectives, such as *tall, taller, tallest.*

Preschoolers amass a larger repertoire of helping verbs, such as *could, must, might, were.* They rarely use two at a time, however, as in "I *could have* finished that." Three-year-olds probably grasp *can't, don't, isn't, won't,* and other simple negative helping verbs. By age four, children are using *wasn't, wouldn't, couldn't,* and *shouldn't.* At the same time, they are learning negative noun forms such as *nobody, no one,* and *nothing.* It is common for children to combine two negatives, as in "I didn't do nothing." Preschoolers start to use helping verbs to form grammatical questions, like "Can I play now?" More challenging questions involving negatives or demanding more than a yes/no answer can cause them to misplace the helping verb: "Why I can't have ice cream?"

In constructing sentences, four-year-olds begin using clauses, not simply adjectives, to modify their nouns. They usually start working on the objects of their sentences: "I liked the monkey that swung on a rope," but not "The monkey that swung on a rope was funny." Preschoolers also start building compound sentences: "I want corn *because* it tastes better than lima beans." However, a sentence like "Before we eat dinner, you should wash your face," can confound a young child because the action she should do first comes second. She could more easily understand, "Wash your face before we eat dinner."

In their preschool years, children start to spot patterns in how words change to indicate different meanings. They hear how adding -er sometimes turns a verb into the person who does that act: teach, teacher. It also indicates more: big, bigger. They realize that adding -ed to a verb means the action took place in the past, but they often forget the irregular verbs, such as came, went, and saw. Preschoolers thus run up against a fact that both frustrates and fascinates linguists: no natural language follows a completely consistent set of rules.

Because children over the age of three grasp simple patterns of sentence structure, they do much better at understanding what adults say to them. At this age, they hear the difference between "The dog is feeding Daddy" and "Daddy is feeding the dog," and are no longer guided by the most likely scenario. As with past tenses, preschoolers tend to overgeneralize the rules they know. Having learned that a subject usually comes first in a sentence, a child may well understand a statement like, "The dog is being fed by Daddy" as meaning that a dog is feeding her father. Children do not usually grasp the passive voice until they are seven.

Preschoolers can explore a single topic at greater length than before. They have also come to understand that words in one sentence refer to a previous sentence. Thus, a four-year-old can say, "I have an uncle named John. He rides a bicycle. Aunt Annie does, too." In this sequence, "he" refers back to Uncle John and "does" to riding a bicycle. A younger child would not have been able to put those sentences together. If a toddler says, "I went to Grandma's for dinner," and you ask, "Where did you go?" he probably has to repeat the whole sentence. A four-year-old can usually pick out the specific fact you asked for and say, "To Grandma's."

Most importantly, in the preschool period, children begin to use language for a much wider range of functions, such as reasoning, solving problems, making friends, narrating events, and playing imagination games. Toddlers use language as a system for mapping what they see and do, especially in communication with their parents and other caregivers. For preschoolers, it is an instrument of thought: their cognitive, language, and social skills become closely entwined. (See Chapter 9 on friends.)

Language grows into a preschooler's primary tool in building and maintaining social relationships.

Because preschoolers are becoming more sophisticated about how people use language, caregivers can introduce new concepts in etiquette. For instance, you might teach your students that they have an outside voice for calling across a playground and a quieter inside voice for speaking to you and to friends in the classroom. You may even teach them to have an extra-quiet library voice they can use when they do not want to bother the people around them, as in a theater. As they start school, many children benefit from hearing that teachers will expect them to use particular styles of conversation in class. In families who speak two or more languages, children learn when each is most appropriate; if they will use one language in school, they need to know that.

Along with all these discoveries, preschool children learn they can use language to explore language itself. This metalinguistic awareness takes many forms. A little girl might come up with new words just for fun: "This place is 'snakey' because it has snakes." A four-year-old boy may insist, while playing a game, that his playmates use particular words because he knows that language can create a new reality: "You're the baby, so you call me 'Daddy.'" Preschoolers start to be interested in rhymes as they realize that words similar in one way (sound) can be distinct in another (meaning). And, as we will discuss in the next chapter, during this period, children discover one of the most powerful things that can be done with words: they are not only spoken, hence fleeting, but can be written down, hence saved.

WRAP IT UP

Parents and caregivers around the world speak to their infants in similar ways that stimulate more frequent and more sophisticated speech. As language and communication skills develop steadily in the first three to five years, they draw children and caregivers closer together.

Even before they start talking, infants engage in a great deal of communication. Far from being a blank slate, an infant acts to hold adults' attention and elicit positive responses. Being able to attract an adult's attention, maintain a social relationship, and inspire affection, helps an infant survive.

At each stage in a young child's life, caregivers naturally seem to communicate in the way that best encourages new language skills. The average child says her first word and her first step around the time of her first birthday. In the second year, a remarkable time for a child's language development, children's first words foreshadow their grasping the idea that objects have names and that other people understand those names. Toddlers will begin to speak in sentences, but typically, the sentences reflect their interests and limitations. In vocabulary, a toddler probably understands three times as many words as they use.

Preschoolers, by the middle of their fourth year, can express themselves much like adults. Preschoolers vocabularies are growing fast. They can pick up new words at an astonishing rate of nine per day. This is also the time when children begin to explore the rules of language. They can use language to indicate ownership of a specific toy. They can convey that something is in the past or an event is yet to come. They learn words for expressing themselves in time, they can ask and answers questions, and their sentences now include clauses.

Most importantly, in the preschool period, children begin to use language for a much wider range of functions, such as reasoning, solving problems, making friends, narrating events, and playing imagination games. Because preschoolers are becoming sophisticated about how people use language, teachers can introduce new concepts in etiquette. For example, to use an outside voice on the playground and a quieter inside voice for speaking in the classroom. Amid all of these discoveries, preschool children learn they can learn to use language to explore language itself. They may invent new words or insist on using specific words in pretend play. They are interested in rhymes as they realize that words can be similar in sound but can be distinct in meaning.

CHAPTER 6

Literacy Growth and Milestones

The joy of literacy, from reading to storytelling to writing to playacting, can become the center of your preschool classroom.

Until the early nineteenth century, only the privileged—wealthy families, professionals, clerics—had formal education and were literate. Books were not widely available, and information was often delivered through stories, speeches, or newspapers read aloud by a literate member of the community or family member. Family and community stories were preserved by an oral instead of a written tradition, and storytellers were prized for their accumulated wisdom and historical memory. With the spread of public education in the early twentieth century and more widely available printed material, not only were people more literate, but reading also became a practical way to convey information: the printed word preserved traditions and stories. While storytellers brought the people in a community together, books made it possible to link multiple communities together to share information and stories, which could travel faster through the printed word. Public libraries ensured that anyone, whether rich or poor, could have access to the same information.

Reading brings adults and children together in a different way than storytelling. As children learn to read, they pick up information and stories they can relate to their parents. They can read along with their parents and learn about traditions from beyond their personal experience. Reading is an essential skill, even as reading on screens has become as common as reading printed material. In fact, the primary means of learning the skills required for every technology is still the written word. The spreading and promoting of ideas increasingly depends on a person's talent at writing, and the ability to easily read is crucial to that talent. Families who read together demonstrate to their children that books are a primary and lifelong source of both learning and pleasure. In this chapter we discuss the importance of reading aloud to children and ways to encourage them to read on their own.

Reading Aloud to a Child

Many of the world's greatest storytellers have described being read to as children. You may have your own memories of intimate moments around bedtime, on the couch, or with the whole family at the supper table reading and telling stories. Stories implicitly involve at least two people: the storyteller and the audience of one or more who listen to it. Telling a story is a social act and a potential act of love. Many cultures have preserved their history through telling stories from generation to generation. Even today, the stories parents tell or read to their children are a major part of what defines the family for them.

The short story master Eudora Welty recalled her mother this way: "She'd read to me in the big bedroom in the mornings, when we were in her rocker together, which ticked in rhythm as we rocked, as though we had a cricket accompanying the story."

Books are crucial to your life as an adult. As a teacher, you encourage childrens' interest in reading in school. You should also be aware of how important it is for a child's development for a caregiver to tell stories and read aloud to her in the years before she can read to herself. First, the ritual of reading aloud to a child shows that reading is a highly valued skill. Second, reading as another mode of communication, produces another dimension of reality that also encourages discussion and imagining. When you or a caregiver reads aloud, asking questions about the book makes the child actively think about the world.

In a sense, through reading aloud, caregiver and child together create what many developmentalists call a shared space. This is the all-important world of make believe and imagination, as we discussed in Chapter 4. Within this space, a caregiver and child develop a shared language unique to the two of them and laden with associations to the stories they have read and told together. References to these books may come up again and again in everyday life. Often adults read to children books they remember from their own childhood, creating or maintaining a tradition.

Reading aloud to children juxtaposes two vivid experiences: the experience related in the story and the experience of reading it together. In the classroom, teachers know how to enhance both experiences by asking the child questions, such as "What happens in the story? What does the character want? Who is he, who could he be? What does he know?"

These do not need to be teaching exercises to see whether the child understands the story; rather, these questions should arise naturally. If a child resists answering or tries to change the subject, back off. He may be so caught up in the story that he just wants to find out what comes next.

A child may come to believe she can be just like that brave child in the story or be comforted to find that she and a character share difficult feelings, such as Jo's anger in *Little Women*. Children can also make value judgments about characters and their actions. By exploring such issues with a child, you help her create her sense of herself. Reading gives a child the feeling that she knows something special, something she has learned with you or, as she comes to read herself, on her own.

Caregivers and children who share reading aloud come to share not only similar frames of reference, memories, and mental associations, but also values. Thus, as a child gets older, teachers and parents can use stories and books to convey the values you would like children to think about and absorb from you. Stories that are not about a child's immediate world can provide a psychologically safe way of addressing personal choices and fears. Through stories, you can encourage a child to imagine what else might have happened. Through fiction, children can witness emotions and traumatic situations that they may one day face in real life but hopefully not when they are young, such as the death of a pet or a beloved person, the upheaval of war, the temptation of risky behavior. But stories need not be fictional; you may read a biography or true account to your children, especially if you enjoy this type of reading. The essence of reading aloud is putting feeling into words, letting children sit close and listen to information conveyed verbally, and encouraging them to bring their own feelings and responses to the experience.

Finally, stories are themselves a sort of metaphor—a tale of something that usually did not happen but might have, at least within some version of reality. A child naturally identifies with characters his own age or a little older (the age he envisions himself being soon). At the same time, he knows that he is *not* the child in the story; on reflection he can identify ways in which he is different. Reviewing the stories he hears helps a child play with the differences between "me" and "other people," between "real" and "pretend." One day a child may tell you he is a character from a book, and the next day he may decide he's not like that character at all. Stories let young children try on some grown-up roles through identification with animal characters as well. Winnie the Pooh lives in his own house like an adult, but his emotions and intellect are more like those of a child. Young readers who can easily relate to Pooh can thus imagine what it would be like to live on their own, without the frightening thought of actually having to do so. Fiction gives children a safe setting to explore answers to questions they may not have considered yet.

> *Children learn that in books they can find answers to many vital questions, learn new things, and think through events that bother them.*

Can a Child Read Too Much?

You can have too much of a good thing—even of reading—and a child can read too much. It is not that too much reading harms vision, as people sometimes fear. Even reading under the covers with a flashlight is an encouraging sign of your child's enthusiasm for books, not a cause for major worry. In general, voracious reading is a cause for celebration and rarely a sign for concern.

However, there are some situations in which the amount of time a child spends reading may be a problem because of the time it takes away from other activities, especially if important areas of development are being neglected. A school-age child may be reading too much when that activity cuts into other crucial developmental tasks, such as engaging with the real world and developing social skills, or avoiding physical activities and neglecting those skills. In these cases, it bears looking at whether reading is precluding activities or signaling other issues.

If you think one of your students is an avid reader, encourage her to take action. A child who likes science books may be lured into building model rockets. You can also encourage your students to write their own stories or create role-playing games around well-known characters to play with their friends.

Why Read to a Child
Who Cannot Yet Speak?

Experts recommend that parents start reading to their children within a few weeks of birth. Reading stories to infants serves many purposes. At its simplest level, it provides intimate time together, with child and parent sitting still and close. A ritual of reading, most often after dinner and before sleeping, gives parent and child a regular quiet, relaxed time. Reading aloud is a task both parents can share equally. While a father cannot breastfeed, he can enjoy the intimate experience of holding his new baby in his arms as he reads a story. Reading aloud with children is also one of the best ways to bring an older sibling and a new baby together, with the former sitting close beside while her parent holds the baby and reads. The older sibling has the pleasure of understanding that she knows what is happening in the book while the baby does not. But babies still benefit from listening. Reading aloud conveys not just the words, but the emotions of the story and the rhythm of language. Even if a baby cannot understand their content, books bring babies and parents together.

Yet another benefit of reading to infants is that it establishes the routine of reading aloud, which continues as children grow up. This social interaction between parent and child is as developmentally important as the story they are reading. Particularly for babies, what is important is the emotional experience: being with a parent, hearing her voice, watching her face, seeing her changing facial expressions. A parent can even read the sports page aloud to a one-month-old in her arms. Victories and defeats, batting averages read with feeling—those can begin to define the space for reading together.

Nursery rhymes and songs are especially good for babies because they have rhythm, often repeating sounds and phrases in regular fashion, and the simple verses encourage the reader to play with his or her voice in a way that is particularly appropriate for infants. Nursery rhymes and lullabies are part of a family's heritage, sometimes passed down for generations. In the broad sense of literacy, songs are a form of shared storytelling. Their playfulness is appropriate for appeals to very young children, who are themselves playing with language and babbling nonsensical words.

Everyone has a reading voice, whether they realize it or not. This voice usually exaggerates the feelings conveyed in a story, pauses at dramatic moments, and signals breaks through changes in tone and volume. Sometimes, when the reader is really into the story, he changes his voice to suit particular characters. What teacher has not tried to sound like a gruff bear grumbling about a cold bowl of porridge? Infants

sometimes react with wide eyes the first time they hear such voices, but a parent's closeness reassures them that this is just another way people communicate. Some adults feel self-conscious about reading expressively, but there is no better time to growl than when you are reading *Goldilocks and the Three Bears*, and no better audience to appreciate your efforts than a class full of children.

A Different Sort of Language

Is it necessary to read from a book, you may ask, to gain all these benefits? After all, a caregiver can make up a story, or tell one from memory, and enjoy closeness with a child while introducing him to language. Many children like nothing better than to hear stories about their own parents or other caregivers as children, recalled on the spot. Improvising a story or adding to a story developed between you and your students will have many of the same benefits as reading. Parents and children also benefit from watching television shows or videos together and discussing the characters, action, and issues the stories raise. All of these forms are components of a rich and varied culture of literacy.

However, none of these experiences exactly replicates the benefits of reading aloud from storybooks. The difference goes beyond the method and the pace of the storytelling. It has to do with the language of written stories and the way young minds learn to process that language.

A written story always flows differently from a spoken story, no matter how skilled the storyteller. Written text contains the "he said" and "she said" tags as conventions to mark a conversation; these are not available, and not needed, when a person hears two different voices conversing. Even newspaper accounts of that final game in the World Series sound different from the plays as called by the announcers, with the pauses, excitement, and ignorance about the outcome. When you talk with another person, you convey a great deal of information nonverbally through facial expressions, hand gestures, and other physical cues. Your listeners follow your incomplete sentences, shifts of tense or reference, or even topic changes because of nonverbal signals such as gestures, alterations in tone, or body language. The writer of a story must, through marks on a page, convey all of these signals clearly enough to give a reader the feeling of listening to a particular conversation even if the author invented it. Listening to written text read aloud gives children of all ages experience with language in different forms and rhythms. Preschoolers who have listened to a caregiver read them a great number of books are more likely to speak in sentences of complex structure than children who learn language only through conversation. Children who are early readers and who come to school with beginning reading skills are similarly those who have been read to at home.

Through stories read aloud, children expand their vocabulary and their sense of the variety of language. Many stories for children are filled with dialects and other ways of speaking that may be new to a child's ears. Even stories about real figures or places expand a child's worlds imaginatively. Through reading, children can imagine what it was like to live in the distant past or a far-off location, or even to be a teacher meeting a new class of students.

Reading aloud to children can expand their vocabulary and accelerate their language acquisition.

By reading aloud to children, you, as a teacher, provide another means of learning about language. You teach them pronunciation and how words combine to convey a scene, feeling, or experience. You show how language can shift from the concrete to the metaphorical. Such metaphors as "hard rain" and "feeling blue" appear in everyday spoken language, but a story usually links more images and establishes associations. Language builds on what developmentalists call cross-modal perception, or experiencing something from one mode of sensation, such as hearing, in another mode, such as touch or vision. Listening to a story read aloud is itself a cross-modal experience. It arouses a child's imagination so that, through her ears alone, she is able to experience the events of the book.

The Timing and Technique of Reading Aloud

Parents and caregivers can read to a child any time the mood strikes. In a classroom, there is likely a scheduled time for reading, but try to make yourself available for reading during free play time. For most young children, about fifteen minutes a day is the ideal amount of listening time, so make sure you schedule enough time. Make sure the place where you gather to read is reasonably free of distractions. Everyone should be comfortable—children and teacher together—and not rushed. If you are trying to get the story over with so you can move on to the next task on the schedule, the experience loses some of its closeness and relaxing satisfaction.

What you read to the children in your class will vary according to their ages and your own tastes. Through the classroom or school library, you can experiment with different books for your students. If you do not like a particular nursery rhyme or book, your lack of enjoyment and engagement will diminish the experience for your students. Therefore, pick something you enjoy reading.

For babies, the content does not matter; it is the experience of being together that counts. As a child nears eighteen months, he starts to enjoy the simplest picture books. Stories that repeat a given scene or refrain over and over are particularly attractive to a toddler. The rhythm of recurring scenes promises a constancy to the world—the same reassurance a child seeks in her bedtime ritual. Thus, a child often insists on hearing the same story night after night.

By age three, children are ready for stories about imaginary events, rather than just about lives like their own. Books that tell a story with pictures and only a small amount of text are best for preschoolers because they can participate in telling the story as they look at the pictures. With familiar stories, you can ask your students about the events of the story. You can play "I spy" as you explore the pages of richly illustrated picture books. This game does not require books with hidden pictures—those are challenges for older children (and adults). Researchers listening to parents read to their older toddlers estimate that the family spends only half of their time reading from the pages; the other half is filled with conversation about the book.

Children entering kindergarten and the first grade are able to enjoy stories that rely on words more than on pictures. They develop the ability to imagine and create their own mental images to illustrate the tales or bridge the gap between drawings. (See Chapter 4 for

more on imagination.) Their memory has also become more powerful, and they can delay the gratification of hearing how a story turns out. Children of this age are ready to hear you tell a story in short chapters, reading one each day. The earliest chapter books are really collections of short stories involving the same characters; each installment is satisfying in itself, and the child can anticipate the return of a familiar cast the next day. Chapter books for slightly older readers have stories that continue from one chapter to the next, building suspense. The story, and your pleasure in reading together, establish continuity from day to day.

There are many benefits to reading aloud to children even after they start reading by themselves. It can help pass the time and preserves the sense of closeness that caregivers and children both enjoyed when they were younger. Reading books together demonstrates a continued interest in what children are learning and in reading itself. Some children may resist if they become busier or believe they are too old for reading aloud. In this case, parents and caregivers can find books more engaging or appropriate to the child's age. If reading aloud is not possible, families should replace the read-aloud time with other activities related to reading, to maintain that close bond. In the preschool years and beyond, reading aloud continues to serve a central role for both literacy building and shared classroom community.

Helping Children to Read on Their Own

For many parents, hearing their child read a story from beginning to end for the first time is as exciting as watching him take his first step. Many adults can still remember the plot of the first book they read as a child. This milestone opens up a whole new world for the child, and parents and caregivers realize that they will no longer be the source of all his stories. Although some children learn to read before kindergarten, most enter school knowing only the letters of the alphabet, and some have not acquired even that much. (See "Parents' Roles in Supporting Children with Learning Disabilities" on pages 118–119.) Children learn to read primarily in school, but when their parents instill literacy at home, it makes it easier for you to teach them. Select reading material that matches your students' developmental levels and interests, which may require a broad range of books. When possible, give your students the time and space to read at school, and make time to read to them as well. As children get older, teachers will assign books for school assignments, so preschool teachers and families can teach young children that reading is a pleasure even when it is not required.

Parents can start early by providing their infant with one or two books made of durable, perhaps even washable, materials. They can let her play with these as she would play with any other toy. The point is not to have her reading before she turns two, but she might start to imitate how an adult turns the pages of regular books. The value of such toys is in showing young children that books are part of everyday life, and that some books belong to them alone.

Because toddlers love to listen to stories from books that play with sounds, when they hear a simple, well-conceived text over and over, they start to connect what is on each page with the sounds they hear. Pointing to the words and pictures reinforces this knowledge. Good books for toddlers include vocabulary books that show one object and word at a time, storybooks, and board books with colorful pages.

In preschool, children like to put things in order. The alphabet is an appealing plaything, in the form of alphabet blocks, felt toys, and colorful magnets. Show a child how to draw the first letter of her name, and send it home for her parents to see. Use letters in the activities you plan, teaching the children how to draw letters and discussing the words that begin with a given letter. Keep crayons and paper handy, not just for drawing but for "writing." Hang labels around the room to identify objects and ask students to locate a particular letter.

The preschool years are also the time to introduce your students to the school library and encourage parents and caregivers to take their children to the public library, whether for borrowing books or other activities.

In the library, a child should participate in choosing the books. When possible, allow your students to choose a book to read at school or to take home. Preschoolers can discuss their likes and dislikes, so you can help them find books that capture their interest if they are not able to find them on their own.

If you read a favorite book to your students often enough, you can pause two or three words before the end of a sentence and let them fill in the rest. This cooperation engages the preschoolers with the storytelling by drawing on their natural desire for consistency. You could also try substituting a silly word for a word your students know belongs in the story. Such techniques are both more fun and more effective than halting the flow of the story for a reading lesson ("See, that spells 'horse.' H is for 'horse.'. . ."). By filling in the right words, your students are not necessarily reading in the sense of recognizing a word by sight outside its familiar context; they are, however, demonstrating their knowledge that there are words on that page and that reading is the process of getting them right. They are also participating in shared reading, an important element of literacy development.

By creating a classroom that values books and makes letters a pleasant part of daily life, you help your students want to read.

The First R: Reading in School

Learning to read in school is a different experience from learning to read at home. The child is now in a large group, with less individual attention and adjustment for his own interests, skills, and emotional state. Schools provides systemic teaching aimed at instilling systematic reading skills. For most children, they are successful. Typical first-graders can read only about 100 words, though their spoken vocabularies include around 6,000. Three years later, children can usually read 100 words each minute, recognize 3,000 words at a glance, and apply over 100 rules for sounding out the words they do not know. If all continues to go well, by age fifteen students should recognize 100,000 words quickly and read more than 200 words a minute. (See "Literacy Milestones.")

Literacy Milestones

As with other developmental milestones, those relating to literacy arrive in a specific order over a range of time. Here is a summary of the literacy milestones.

Age	Reading and Writing Milestones	Types of Books
6 to 12 months	Holds and drops books; likes books with baby faces and rhythmic reading	Board books, cloth books, picture books with baby faces, nursery rhymes
12 to 24 months	Holds books; turns pages of board books; asks to be read to; follows along; names pictures	Board books, picture books, books that teach identification, books that rhyme
2 to 3 years	Turns pages a few at a time; begins scribbling; likes hearing familiar stories repeatedly	Picture books with stories, books that rhyme, books with objects to find or identify
3 to 4 years	Turns pages one at a time in the right order; enjoys longer stories; scribbles and draws; starts recognizing letters; pretends to read	Longer picture books, books with objects to find or identify
4 to 5 years	Copies letters and numbers; enjoys even longer stories; recognizes letters and sounds; can retell stories	Longer stories with fewer pictures, fantasy stories

For many years, much attention has been paid to methods of teaching reading, especially "whole language" versus "phonics." The whole language approach focuses on literature and meaning through immersion in a written language. In this model, a child learns the sound/symbol system through exposure to several types of written materials. On the other hand, the phonetic approach focuses on giving students the skills they need to crack the code. Students receive direct instruction on the relationship between letters and their sounds and are taught how to blend sounds sequentially to make words.

Most reading teachers believe that the best lesson plan combines several techniques. Children do benefit from learning pronunciation guidelines. Unfortunately, English is a large and inconsistent language, with so many phonics rules (well over one hundred) and so many exceptions to them (about one in every three words) that trying to learn them all can leave students discouraged or bored. Preserving and extending children's early love of reading is why whole-language lessons emphasize literature and self-expression. Sticking to either method exclusively, however, seems to work for only a fraction of students. Even worse, having to shift abruptly after changing grades or schools can leave children confused about what their teachers expect. That is why a good mix of methods is best. The most important factor in learning to read is the amount of time a student spends with books in school and at home. You can help by encouraging parents to read to their children at home to ensure that reading remains a pleasurable part of their child's daily life.

As a student becomes more proficient with books, encourage him to read simple, familiar stories aloud to you and other students. Your goal in these moments is not to review word recognition, pronunciation, or elocution, but to give the student the pleasure of mastery: now *he* is telling the story he loves. When he comes across a word that he does not recognize but is in his spoken vocabulary, encourage him to sound it out. When he meets a completely unfamiliar word, however, read and explain it. Some children may not want to read aloud at school. You can encourage parents and caregivers to try this at home, where it should be acceptable for a young reader to make mistakes. Reading at home will give him the practice and confidence he needs for reading at school.

A picture book for a beginning reader should have enough text that a child becomes immersed in each page and doesn't flip quickly to the next. On the other hand, if a child stumbles or needs help five times while reading one page, she is not yet ready to handle that book on her own. Beyond those criteria, a "good book" for a child is one that appeals to her interests and tastes. Most kids enjoy stories about children like themselves (and a little bit older) or about childlike animals. Preschoolers are often ready to explore more fantastic situations and settings, such as outer space, the high seas, and fairyland. Humor grabs almost every child. Familiar characters from television have great appeal, and harnessing this fondness may encourage children to read more. If a child still resists reading on his own, do not assume you need better books. Look around for what else could make reading enticing, based on the child's interests, such as reading directions for a board game.

Some parents are so eager to help their children read that they invest in educational aids, tools, and software in addition to books. The value of such products varies, but none is a substitute for simple encouragement. Rather than buying flash cards to teach new words, families can make their own. In addition to "sight words," those simple, common words that children recognize by sight, parents and teachers can let them choose words that will appeal to them, such as the names and species of their stuffed animals or objects from their favorite picture books.

Make sure your classroom has a good dictionary and make a point of looking up words that are new to students. Computers with educational software and multimedia encyclopedias are useful, but they can become expensive substitutes for television or a video game system. (See "Children and Computers.")

Most children become proficient readers after the fourth grade. Over the next few years, it can be hard to keep up with all the books these youngsters consume. But it is still important for caregivers to stay involved in a child's reading selections by asking questions about his choices and listening to his recommendations about good stories.

Children and Computers

One important responsibility that parents and teachers have is preparing children to work effectively in a computerized world. Applying principles of child development to teaching computer literacy can make the choices easier. For instance, we know that toddlers are interested in doing things they see their parents doing. Seeing a parent focusing attention on a smartphone, computer, or tablet makes the toddler want to do the same thing. Some software and apps are designed for parents and children to use together. Adapted to a youngster's lack of fine motor skills (see Chapter 3), these programs often respond any time the child presses a key or touches the screen. She can also point to the screen while a parent taps the touchscreen or clicks the mouse.

Educational software for older children should match their level of development. At ages two to four, children work on motor and cognitive skills. With widely available software or apps, they can practice distinguishing colors and shapes, naming objects, combining images and letters, and producing a tangible product that they can take home to put on their refrigerator door. In early elementary school, children learn how to read, write, and master mathematics, so their technology should let them practice these skills. As with toys and books, if you do have computers or tablets available for your students, make sure you have a variety of software choices to suit different interests and learning styles.

Because personal computers are beyond some families' means, making them available at school is particularly helpful for those children.

Children become interested in video games at a young age, and they're available on a broad range of platforms and in numerous genres. Many focus on quick reactions, memory skills, puzzle solving, or other critical thinking challenges. The games offered on school devices should be educational but fun. As children reach the middle grades, they tend to lose interest in the educational games in favor of whatever game is most popular at the time.

Due to the COVID-19 pandemic, children had to shift to learning via computer at home while their schools were closed to in-person learning. Teachers taught remotely, through group and one-on-one video chats or written lessons. Keeping the connection with students became harder, but many students were better able to adapt because they were already comfortable using technology. Many children grow up with computer technology and the internet, and mastering daily video chats did not require much adjustment. Many may have already used video chats to keep in touch with distant relatives. Just as earlier generations grew up accustomed to everyday technologies like cars, television, or desktop computers, today's children take modern technology for granted and consider it both ordinary and essential.

The Fourth-Grade Slump

Those avid, budding readers you see in preschool and early elementary often, despite the best efforts of caregivers and educators, give way to a reading slump in later elementary school. While most students continue to progress at a fast pace, many others—one in every three or four—slow down. They do not become illiterate or stop learning new words, nor are they necessarily suffering from reading disabilities. (See Chapter 7.) Rather, these students simply become less interested in reading, a trend that continues as they grow older. According to one National Assessment of Educational Progress survey, about half of American fourth-graders reported reading for pleasure, but only one-quarter of twelfth-graders did. Not only does this large minority fall behind their peers as adolescence progresses, they also often fail to gain an important new set of reading skills. Kids in elementary school tend to read at only one speed, taking in all the information uncritically: if it's in a book, it must be true. In high school, students learn which passages to focus on and which to zip over, reading quickly. They also learn to approach books critically, considering the relative merits of a novel or which perspective they should believe.

Researchers have suggested several explanations for the slump that begins around fourth grade. The reading material itself becomes more challenging. For the first time, students face texts with vocabulary and sentence structure more demanding than those in an average conversation. Books have fewer pictures and less familiar subjects, which can excite some students but intimidate others. Teaching methods also change. Lessons focus on writing, not reading. In-class assignments tend to require silence and faster mental processing of the words. Homework gives students more to read for school, and thus less time to devote to reading of their own choice. Children in the late elementary grades have many demands on their time as they become more active socially and try new hobbies. All of these changes probably diminish some children's pleasure in reading. In addition, the fact that around this time both parents and teachers tend to stop reading aloud to children may devalue books in some youngsters' eyes.

Boys seem to suffer the fourth-grade slump more than girls do. One reason may be that boys may feel social pressure not to read widely, or at all. They are often reluctant to be seen reading a book with a girl as the main character, while most girls remain open to stories about boys. Boys are also less interested in certain genres, especially historical fiction (unless it involves battles) and romance. They may shift their reading to nonfiction books, science fiction, and other socially popular forms. Many boys simply divert their energy toward other interests like computers, movies, or sports. As a preschool teacher, you may feel that there is not much you can do about the fourth-grade slump. Even so, make sure you continually promote the value of reading and keep reading to your students. You may well be laying the groundwork for habits that will lead to a lifelong love of reading and later success.

Preserving a Reading Tradition

In present-day American society, people seem to have less time for long stories that unfold over time. Information often arrives in short, staccato bits conveyed from an impersonal organization electronically via television or the internet. Children mostly learn news, facts, and stories through the mass media, rather than through intimate, face-to-face conversation with the family. Increasingly, children take in news, facts, and stories on their own. Seldom are parents close by to provide explanations and frameworks and to encourage them to react to and think about what they have just heard and seen.

Reading can help bridge that gap by bringing people and families together and encouraging imagination. As we have emphasized, this is the social and developmental value of reading—an activity that caregivers and children can share and whose benefits are lifelong. While quantities of information will continue to pour in electronically to American homes and classrooms, it is unlikely that reading, as a basic skill taught early in school, will disappear. Helping your students learn the value of communicating through the written word will facilitate their ability to understand the difference between quick and simplistic information exchange and complex stories and conversations. As they appreciate reading as a means of bringing people together, they will also appreciate the written word as a means to expand and deepen thought.

WRAP IT UP

Reading brings adults and children together in a different way than storytelling. As children learn to read, they pick up information and stories they can relate to their parents. They can read along with their parents and learn about traditions from beyond their personal experience. Reading is an essential skill, even as reading on screens has become as common as reading printed material.

Experts recommend that parents start reading to their children within a few weeks of birth. Reading stories to infants establishes the routine of reading aloud, which continues as children grow up. This social interaction between parent and child is as developmentally important as the story they are reading. Particularly for babies, what is important is the emotional experience: being with a parent, hearing her voice, watching her face, seeing her changing facial expressions.

By reading aloud to children, a preschool teacher provides another means of learning about language by teaching children pronunciation and how words combine to convey a scene, feeling, or experience. A teacher shows how language can shift from the concrete to the metaphorical.

Parents can introduce their infants to books by providing books made of durable materials. They can let her play with these as she would play with any other toy. The point is not to have her reading before she turns two, but she might start to imitate how an adult turns the pages of regular books.

In preschool, along with reading aloud to children, teachers can encourage literacy by providing alphabet blocks, felt toys, and colorful magnets. A teacher can bring children to the library and encourage them to pick out books that they would like to read at home or at school.

As children are beginning to learn to read, most reading teachers believe that the best reading plan combines several techniques: learning pronunciation guidelines and reading books to encourage a love of books and reading. As children get older, most kids enjoy stories about children like themselves (and a little bit older) or about childlike animals. Preschoolers are often ready to explore more fantastic situations and settings, such as outer space, the high seas, and fairyland. Humor grabs almost every child. For children who resist reading, encourage them to read something they would find enticing, like the directions of a board game. Most children become proficient readers after fourth grade, though sometimes, the avid, budding readers of preschool and early elementary school—mostly boys—give way to a slump in fourth grade.

In present-day American society people seem to have less time for reading long stories that unfold over time. Short bits of information on television and on the internet will continue to pour into American homes and classrooms. Helping children learn the value of communicating through the written word will facilitate their ability to understand the difference between a quick and simplistic information exchange and complex stories and conversations.

CHAPTER 7

Partnering with Families

School readiness involves more than knowing colors or the alphabet. The child, family, and even the teacher have a host of social and emotional needs to address in order to be ready for a successful first school experience.

❝**T**om's first day of kindergarten was just a mess of contradictions," his mother says. "For both him and me. I woke up, all jittery, and I couldn't tell if I was excited or anxious. I had to fix Tom his favorite breakfast, pack his lunch, wake him up, and make sure he was dressed right without all his hair sticking up. And all the while, I was sure I'd have to be reassuring him that he'd have a fine day. I went to Tom's bedroom, half wishing I could just let my little angel sleep, and he opens the door. My regular sleepyhead was fully dressed, backpack and all! And he asks me, 'Is the school bus here yet?'

"'It will be here soon,' I said. 'Let's eat breakfast first!' I watched him run downstairs, all the while thinking: Wasn't it just last year that Tom went down these stairs backward, one step at a time? It seems like last week that he—'Where's breakfast, Mommy?' Tom called. The next hour seemed to pass in a blaze. Before I knew it, I was walking and Tom was *running* toward the bus stop at the end of the street. The big yellow bus rounded the corner. Suddenly I felt little fingers clamp onto my hand. 'I don't want to go to kindergarten,' Tom pleaded. My heart ached as I started that reassuring speech I had planned. The bus pulled to a stop. We spot two familiar little faces from Tom's day care peering out. And before I could kiss my baby good-bye, he was on the bus. 'Bye, Mommy!'"

Parents may be torn between happiness and sadness when their child disappears into the school bus or classroom for the first time. Their child will be experiencing excitement and anxiety, delight and dread, courage and fear, and his parents will be too. In fact, these contrasting feelings will remain all along the path toward independence that their child begins to follow on that first day of school. This challenging journey requires many new cognitive, social, and emotional skills. And for what could be the first time, children will be learning these skills not only from their parents but from you and their peers.

Starting school is a big step. It is a crucial developmental transition that lays a foundation for adulthood. Many adult measures of success—profession, financial security, healthy relationships, are linked to how well a child masters the tasks of formal education. In this chapter, we review how to help children enjoy a successful journey through school.

Starting School

A child will be ready for formal education only when he or she has developed adequately both socially and physically, as well as cognitively.

For most children, formal education begins with kindergarten. Preschool and other programs, however rigorous their educational activities may be, are still preparation for elementary school. While you can help a child read at age three, or help her adjust emotionally to spending much of the day away from her family, no one can hurry overall development. You can, of course, provide emotional support as she makes the transition to her new tasks.

Ready or Not

Determining a child's school readiness may be difficult for educators and parents and requires careful consideration. Even children who are used to spending their whole day in childcare programs will have to make significant adjustments when they enter kindergarten. Although preschoolers have learned to deal with separation from their parents and to play with other children in a large group, their kindergarten teacher will expect them to behave even more maturely.

As you consult with parents about when to send their child to school, consider several factors. Think about both the child's chronological age and her developmental age. A child's chronological age is her literal age as determined by her birth date, while developmental age refers to how old she "acts," in the sense of her cognitive, social, and language development. Developmental age is not a measure of intelligence. A child who is developmentally young for her age may have superior intelligence, but not yet the social skills, self-control, or attention span necessary for kindergarten. For some children, chronological and developmental age may be equivalent. Others may act old or young for their age. Schools determine kindergarten eligibility based on chronological age: any children who turn five before a specific cutoff point are eligible. This is an easy and unambiguous measure. But as an educator, you know that

developmental age is also important. A child old enough for kindergarten is not necessarily ready to benefit from it. This is especially common for children whose birthdays put them near the cutoff date in their district.

Kindergarten-ready children are expected to have a basic set of capacities to build new skills in the structured environment of the classroom. A kindergarten-ready child should be able to follow simple instructions, attend to a teacher's presentation, express her needs and concerns understandably, share materials with other children, and play in groups. A child's developmental age and readiness can be assessed through a comparison of her cognitive, motor, attention, social, and language skills to those of other children. Observe a child playing and interacting with others, whether other children or adults he doesn't know. Can they understand his speech? Does he listen to others and not interrupt? If he hasn't yet developed these social skills, that doesn't necessarily mean he is not yet ready for school. But a professional assessment of his readiness might be in order.

As a preschool teacher, you can help parents find resources for assessing their children's readiness. Many school districts offer kindergarten screenings. For difficult cases, psychological assessment may be useful. Don't underestimate your intuition and that of the parents, who are the best judge of when a child is ready to start school.

Helping Children Adjust to School

Even if a child meets the school readiness criteria, he may not make the transition smoothly. Perhaps the most common difficulty is separation anxiety. (For more on this emotional experience, see Chapter 8.) For many children, preschool is their first extended separation from their family. Children will naturally worry about what will happen to their parents when they are in school, and their parents will feel some anxiety about separating from their children. Even if a child has been going to day care for a year or more, preschool requires him to adjust to a new adult caregiver, a new site, new peers, and new routines. Usually children feel sad about separating from the adult or adults who have been looking after them. (See Chapter 8 for more on children's feelings for their professional caregivers.)

Separation anxiety is different for different children. For some, this distress fades after the first week of school. For others, it persists over time or recurs after a further change or a stressful experience. Managing separation anxiety requires patience and help from the parents. You and

Expect some difficulties as children adjust to school, and be patient and supportive.

the child's parents can talk to her about her worries and reassure her. You can try to come up with ways to ease the separation. For example, a parent might walk the child to her classroom door rather than just dropping her off at the school entrance, or tape a photograph of the family inside her lunch box. Remember that being able to function away from one's family is a necessary developmental task—one that you yourself once achieved. If a child's separation anxiety doesn't abate after four weeks and she is not responding to efforts to ease her anxiety, you may want to recommend that parents consult their pediatrician or a mental health professional.

As you help a child through this transition, be careful not to do things that inadvertently support his separation anxiety. Do not, for example, allow his parent to become a full-time volunteer in your classroom simply because it helps keep him from crying. Classroom helpers are invaluable but you need volunteers who can help the whole class. If a parent is focused on keeping his child calm, you and the class lose out, and the child will still not have learned to deal with separation.

First Grades: Beginning Elementary School

Parents often ask their child, "What did you do today at kindergarten?" The usual answer is—and should be—"I played." The major goal of kindergarten is to prepare students for intensive instruction in the basic academic skills of reading, writing, and arithmetic, and the playthings and games in a kindergarten classroom are mostly designed for that preparation. In addition to readiness skills, children entering first grade must have learned to follow complex instructions, sit at a table or desk for extended periods, complete tasks independently, and inhibit their impulsive behavior. They should have developed the following preacademic skills:

- visual-motor skills, such as cutting a simple design with scissors, drawing simple shapes and figures, and printing crude but recognizable letters with a pencil;

- prereading skills, such as knowing the letters in the alphabet and that those letters have sounds associated with them, but not what the sounds are;

- math skills, such as counting, grouping, and identifying simple patterns.

As you know, schools work on predictable schedules. Students learn what time to expect lunch and recess, and which days are gym days. Teachers' lesson plans map out the entire year, arranged around holidays, extended vacations, and standardized exams. (See pages 110–112 for more on such tests.) Such scheduling is necessary for schools to keep track of and to teach hundreds of children. But this structure also helps reassure young children. They know what is expected of them from day to day and can be confident that adults are helping them.

In first, second, and third grades, children learn the basic skills of reading, writing, and arithmetic. They will likely also be introduced to science, social studies, literature, and the arts. Kindergarten through third grade are the years in which children acquire fundamental academic and social skills. Because children's development varies so much at this young age, some kindergartners are not ready to enter first grade after only one year of preparation. Many schools deal with this variability by providing "K–1" classes, where children work on both kindergarten and first-grade tasks. An additional kindergarten year is not a sign of failure or slow learning but can indicate the need to get a student's development on track. As with readiness for kindergarten itself, both intelligence and social skills are involved.

Reading and Other Types of Literacy

Educators often remark that in the first three years of school, children learn to read; after that, they read to learn. In fact, from the earliest stages of reading, both are true. Children are learning to read in the preschool years, but at the same time, reading helps them learn about the world and others. Similarly, even after they master decoding and become fluent readers, they will continue to hone their comprehension skills throughout their lives.

The building blocks of literacy begin in preschool or before, often with storytelling, reading aloud, and exploring books. The foundational skills involved in learning to read continue to be the focus of most instruction in early elementary school. Literacy is the cornerstone of education. Arithmetic, for instance, depends on understanding the symbols for numbers and functions, a process much like reading letters. (In fact, teaching early math skills simultaneously builds early literacy skills, as some of the same cognitive processes are involved.) For this reason, literacy is the yardstick that parents, students, and teachers use most often to measure success. If a child in the first few years of elementary school is not reading, parents may wonder why. Children

pick up on this concern, trying hard to read the books in the classroom and comparing their progress with their friends'.

Many skills and abilities go into learning to read. Since reading is a language skill, children must start with a fundamental grasp of the purposes and methods of verbal communication. Reading requires learning the associations between sounds and symbols. A competent reader can decode words from their letters and extract the essential message from a written passage using multiple strategies. Sounding out words and using context clues are essential skills for reading and are part of most instructors' teaching methods. Experts agree that whatever specific approach teachers use, children need direct instruction on many reading strategies. (For much more on reading, see Chapter 6.)

Children vary tremendously in when they become readers. A few students begin first grade with solid reading skills. Others need a couple of years of formal instruction before their independent reading skills emerge. There is usually no correlation between when a child learns to read and that child's intelligence. Researchers have shown, for example, that children who learn to read on their own before the age of five are not more intelligent than their peers.

Parents can support the work you do in the classroom by reading to their children regularly, beginning in infancy, and by being involved with their child's teacher and school. Parental involvement is crucial to a student's success.

Writing, mathematics, and learning to observe the world are essential components of a child's elementary-school education. The pace at which children develop writing skills varies from child to child. Writing requires the visual-motor skill of letter and word formation, the ability to memorize spellings, and the capacity to put thoughts into words. From drawing individual letters in print (and later in cursive), young school-age children progress to copying one-word labels, then to writing short sentences, and finally to composing a series of sentences about a particular topic. Some teachers instruct students to write down their stories and thoughts without regard to spelling at first because their spelling skills will eventually catch up to their other skills.

Mathematics for young students means learning basic addition and subtraction facts, as well as logic and reasoning. Becoming literate in math requires memorizing facts like the multiplication table and comprehending the rules that underlie those facts. To help children approach mathematical concepts from as many directions as possible, it is helpful to use manipulatives: blocks, pegs, balances, little items to count, and so on. Although the methods by which children learn have changed over time, 2 + 2 still equals 4. One way to help your students apply their budding mathematical and writing knowledge is to observe plants, animals, and simple science experiments in the classroom.

Many states mandate physical education, and teachers and children alike benefit from letting children burn off their tremendous energy running around the schoolyard. Recently, programs for younger children have been providing fewer recess periods for playing outside and more academic instruction. The change in emphasis reflects advances in understanding of children's learning capacity in formal settings and concerns about teacher liability as they supervise children's unstructured outside play. In school years 2020 and 2021, concerns about the impact of the COVID-19 impact on students led to an increased emphasis on academics over socializing and play time. These changes have come at a cost. When schools cut content that is not considered "core," eliminating play, arts, and other whole-child experiences, teachers and families need to work together to ensure these other areas are addressed somehow in and out of school. For example, one school in rural Tennessee combined math facts with counting laps around a track.

In upper elementary grades, children have structured athletics or gym class; as they learn to compete and cooperate in different games, they develop gross motor skills (see Chapter 3) and social skills. They exercise their fine-motor skills in art class and other school activities, where they write, cut, paste, paint, and sew. Music, art, and computer classes offered by schools can be a great source of joy to students as they discover new talents.

Grades, Retention, and Acceleration

Children in preschool generally advance according to their age, occasionally but rarely being retained in one grade due to achievement metrics. However, as a child progresses to elementary school, her work is evaluated more formally. With this more specific feedback, she can see how many words she spelled correctly or which math problems she got correct. Young school-age children's feelings of competence and value are closely linked to how they think their teacher views them. They are very sensitive to what they perceive as competition and very conscious of social comparisons. You should therefore praise your students when they work hard and comfort and encourage them when they feel disappointed.

Evaluation systems vary by school district and by school. In preschool, your assessment measures may follow a more qualitative continuum. However, by elementary school, many schools use traditional letter or number grades; others use descriptors like "emerging" or "consistently demonstrates." Especially in the elementary grades, report cards may include both academic topics and non-academic skills and behaviors

Making the Cutoff

Acceleration, or skipping a grade, is a possibility at any point in a student's school career, but is infrequent. Skipping pre-kindergarten is more common than skipping other grades. Some parents who consider their four-year-old academically and developmentally advanced may try to enroll their child in kindergarten if her birthday is near their district's age cutoff. Most schools have an assessment to determine kindergarten readiness. Some parents may change schools in order to get the placement they want, if an initial assessment doesn't support acceleration. Parents need to carefully consider whether starting kindergarten at age four is the best option for their child. They should work with his teachers to assess his development in all areas. If he has some particularly advanced skills, he may benefit more from a special lesson plan in the regular classroom or an after-school enrichment program than from being placed in a class with students who are more developed physically and socially. Parents, teachers, and administrators need to consider the child's feelings and overall welfare. It may make the parents proud that their child is doing work two grades above his level, but he may benefit even more from staying with his friends and peers in his own grade.

related to appropriate developmental benchmarks. Generally, by middle school, marking period grades are focused primarily on academic performance. As a teacher, you may emphasize the distinction between achievement and effort, to encourage students who tried as hard as they could and to prod those with superior potential who did not try hard.

Remember that grades are only one way a child can understand his performance in school. Beginning in preschool, you can assemble portfolios of each child's best work or work that demonstrates growth in a particular area. That portfolio will serve to inform future teachers and can be a valuable way for families to look back together and reflect on how much a child has grown.

At the end of every school year, the question arises whether a child is ready to advance to the next grade. Many parents resist retention (being "left back" or "held back") because they, like many educators and children, view repeating a grade as a sign of failure or limited ability. This is a serious misconception. Retention is an opportunity to make a correction for a child whose development in all areas does not match that of his classmates. Because young children's rates of development vary a lot, it is common for a teacher to recommend adjustments up to the first year or two of elementary school.

Family Involvement in the Classroom

When a child begins school, his parents go back to school. They do not become your students, of course, but they become part of the community that defines and supports your school. They pay for its services with their taxes or tuition, and they share responsibility for making our American educational system work for every child. Ideally, families are involved in their own children's educations and advocate for their needs but also champion the needs of the community's children. It's important to remember that when parents "return" to school with their children, they bring with them their own positive and negative experiences of early education.

Involvement is crucial, because tailoring education to a student's unique characteristics, talents, and vulnerabilities requires feedback and support from parents and other caregivers, who know the child best. Parental involvement is crucial for several reasons. It helps improve the overall school climate, linking the institution with the community around it. It helps teachers understand their students better and leads to positive educational reforms. Research has also found that parental involvement supports students' learning and achievement.

However much you may try to provide the maximum benefit to each of your students, you have limited time in any school day and must spread your attention fairly among all the children in a class. A child's caregivers will be the first to know how her individual needs are changing. Some children may require extra help and support in the preschool and early elementary years and then blossom into thriving, competent students. Others may sail along without difficulty until middle school requires a change in course. A child whose parents are meaningfully involved with her school is likely to develop a stronger sense of her academic abilities and enjoy a better learning outcome. When parents work alongside you and your school's administration, the student will feel as though all the people most important to her are united and devoted to supporting her.

Building a Bridge Between Home and School

Even though most parents would agree that they play an important role in their children's learning, they usually don't have a clear idea of how to bridge home and school. You can make suggestions for ways they can build a collaborative relationship with you—by attending parent–teacher conferences, monitoring their child's homework and school progress, and supporting school events in which he participates. With that foundation, you open up communication with parents or caregivers, which allows for collaborative decisions about a child's classroom placement, special educational interventions, or special testing.

A variety of factors may make this collaboration difficult to achieve. Time is a major constraint for working parents. They may feel too busy to become involved in school, or they may have negative attitudes about school because of their own experiences. Try to be flexible with scheduling or consider sending home activity preparation (such as cutting shapes or collating papers) for parents who want to volunteer but are unable to come into the classroom. You can schedule video chats to update parents who have complicated schedules. Families that are adjusting to life in a new culture or face economic challenges may have less energy to put toward their children's schools. Most often, parents simply do not understand how to navigate the educational culture.

Establish open communication with families and keep them updated on classroom events. You may wish to send out a weekly newsletter via e-mail with the week's lessons and suggestions for reinforcing those lessons at home. Reach out to individual families when you have something especially positive to share about their child. When you communicate with families, they will feel more comfortable partnering with you to help all the students in your class succeed.

Cultural issues influence teachers' abilities to communicate with parents. Many of today's teachers are sensitive to cultural differences, but they may not be aware of all the diversity the students represent. For example, in some cultures, parents teach children to show respect by not making eye contact with adults, but in American society, we are trained to consider such behavior to be evasive, rude, or shy. A teacher evaluating a student based on such a misinterpretation may confuse or alienate the child or family.

Finally, make sure to communicate any expectations the school has of parents or caregivers. Encourage parents to attend back-to-school nights, parent-teacher conferences, and appointments to discuss report cards. If parents are unable to attend meetings, you can schedule phone or video conferences or offer appointments after work hours. Many schools encourage parents to participate in other activities, such as providing refreshments for events, coaching, or chaperoning field trips and after-school activities. Some school districts rely on parents' fundraising activities to supplement their budgets. There are numerous opportunities to involve parents, so they can meet other parents, get to know you and their child's other teachers, and share in some of their child's school experience.

Because parents have different interests and schedules, try to provide a variety of volunteer opportunities. Make sure to let them know that the quality of their involvement is much more important than the quantity. If you have a student whose parent has particular skills—model building, cooking, or gardening, for instance—you could incorporate their skill set into a lesson or activity.

There may be parents who become regular presences at your school, volunteering in any way they can. In some schools, parents are official members of the planning and management team, helping to form policies and representing all the parents in the community. Parent leaders become critical allies and help empower others.

The results of positive parental involvement in school are obvious. Fewer serious problems arise because parents and teachers are able to anticipate difficulties and prevent things from getting out of hand. Solutions are easier to identify when schools have more knowledge and resources. And even when a problem does come up, the atmosphere of cooperation makes it easier for educators and parents to handle It together.

Discipline in School

"Discipline" may carry a negative connotation of punishment. And we are not advocates of the types of discipline that may come to mind, including suspension, expulsion, and revoking of recess. In some extreme cases, measures like this may be necessary. But in ordinary circumstances, we use discipline to mean teaching students to follow rules and act appropriately. Students develop discipline in themselves as part of the learning process, and schools use disciplinary systems to ensure a learning-friendly climate. In preschool and the early elementary grades, a teacher usually handles disruptions in her own classroom. In the late elementary and middle-school grades, consequences for poor behavior can become more serious and may involve detention after school or suspension from school. Since school policies vary, make sure that students and parents are aware of the rules at your school.

Children who misbehave often suffer academic difficulties. It can be challenging to understand which problem is the root of the other. A child who feels frustrated, confused, and incompetent at school is more likely to act out in disruptive or destructive ways. And students who are looking to rebel may not try hard at school. Yet there are students who break rules and still do well in their classes and students who struggle academically but have no unusual discipline problems. Ongoing misbehavior demands a response both in and out of school. It alienates a student from his school and is a serious threat to his intellectual and social development. If you find that you are repeatedly disciplining the same student, consult with school administrators and the child's caregivers. If his infractions involve fighting, destroying property, or other violent acts, such consultation is especially important since these could be signs of deeper psychological trouble. (See Chapter 10.)

Let your students know early on that you value their appropriate behavior in school. Praise them when they behave well and show growth. Keep parents updated about their children's behavior and about events that occur in class. When all the adults in a child's life pool their collective wisdom and collaborate, they produce a seamless web of authority. In this ideal situation, parents back up teachers, teachers help parents, and students learn that they can rely on all of you.

Standardized Testing

The United States is a nation obsessed with measuring, comparing, testing, and rating. Just look at all the "Top Ten" lists and the scored questionnaires and tests in magazines (including parenting magazines). Educators use tests to measure student progress, screen for difficulties, diagnose and repair academic problems, and measure the effectiveness of their curricula. Like any scientific measurement, these data are most reliable when comparing groups, such as one student body with another.

Nevertheless, tests are also useful in determining an individual student's aptitudes, strengths, and areas where she needs further work. As with grades and many other aspects of school, understand your own feelings about these exams. Do tests make you feel queasy? Do you see them as a way to show off your knowledge? Or do your feelings fall somewhere in between?

During a child's school career, he will take a number of standardized tests, whether administered to his class, his grade, or all the students in the school. Some are called ability or aptitude tests; others are achievement or mastery tests. Some states mandate that students must pass specific examinations to graduate. College admission tests like the

SAT (Scholastic Aptitude Test) and the ACT (American College Testing assessment) are important enough in some districts that the curriculum includes test preparation courses.

Familiarize yourself with each test students take, what is measured, how often it is administrated, and what the district or state standards are. Parents should receive a letter telling them about the nature of the test and their child's performance. It should have enough information to interpret a test score. Families themselves schedule and pay for the SAT and the ACT, and official information about those tests should come from the administering organizations.

Most children very much want to please their parents by doing well in school. Parents certainly want their children to perform well on standardized tests, but too much enthusiasm can make a child feel pressured and anxious, possibly affecting his performance. Some parents have difficulty hiding their disappointment when their child does not do well. They may encourage her to work harder next time or promise to give her things if she improves. While she will probably try to improve, her efforts may only heighten her anxiety and thus make it harder for her to do better. A few children feel so much stress that they can barely perform at all or even become ill just before an exam.

A relaxed environment in which to do schoolwork, study, and prepare for exams can help a student perform to the best of his ability. If he

appears to be overly anxious about tests, parents can reassure him of their unconditional love and support, and make sure he gets plenty of rest and a good breakfast on the day of the test. After the test, an assurance of parental love and pride goes a long way toward helping him build a positive academic self-concept.

In addition to group-administered exams, some children will be evaluated with individual tests. These may assess intelligence, academic achievement, learning styles, visual-motor development, language, and social and emotional functioning. There is no need to study for such tests, and children should not feel that they are under pressure to pass. Individual testing is usually reserved for children who are not making adequate progress in some area. A parent may request testing for a child whose progress they're concerned about or may have their child tested privately and ask for you or specialists at the school to evaluate the findings. The results of these assessments may be used to design a new way of teaching for that child, as we discuss in the next section.

Special Education and Learning Disabilities

Since the 1970s, federal law has required public school systems to provide for all children in each district, including children with special needs and disabilities. The law mandates that schools provide that education in the least restrictive environment, that the lessons be appropriate and designed to educate, and that any related services a child needs be provided at no cost to the family. Among the conditions that make a child eligible for special education services are speech and language disabilities, learning disabilities, autism spectrum disorder, severe emotional disturbance, intellectual deficits, traumatic brain injury, visual impairments, hearing impairments, orthopedic disabilities, and other health impairments.

School districts are required to provide special education to children who need it, from age three until either their high-school graduation or age twenty-one, whichever comes first.

Some parents know from the time their child is born or shortly afterward that she will need special education. Most children with Down syndrome, for instance, benefit from special classes or from extra help in regular classrooms. For many other families, however, there are no clear signs that a child will need special services or adjustments in her educational program until after she starts school. Sometimes parents become concerned about their child's progress in a specific area, or her general reluctance to go to classes. The student's teacher may be the first to raise the possibility of a learning disability, reporting that a child does not seem to be working up to his potential or is consistently falling behind the other students. Either the parents or the school may develop a plan to meet a child's special educational needs.

It is important to identify learning difficulties early because their effects often worsen with more challenging work. Ongoing difficulties in learning are additive, meaning they may spread to other areas that have not been previously troublesome. A child who has trouble reading will probably have trouble learning other subjects that depend on reading, such as science and history, and may become so anxious about school that she has trouble with mathematics as well. A child may express or mask her frustration about learning through disruptive classroom behavior. Her continued misbehavior in school and difficulty mastering the material may be signs of emotional problems or a learning disability, and distinguishing among these possibilities requires an evaluation with a psychologist or other specialist. In this section, we aim to explain what it means to be learning disabled and to provide some guidance for teachers with a student who is diagnosed as having a learning disability.

What Learning Disabilities Are—and Are Not

A child who has a learning disability simply has more difficulty than her peers learning the basic skills in school. This difficulty cannot be ascribed to a lack of ability: the child's teacher and parents can see her talents and potential in other areas. Nor does a severe social or emotional problem explain her problems in learning. In fact, this lack of obvious cause partly defines a learning disability—that is, problems with learning that no other factor can account for. A quantitative definition is based on test scores; for a learning disability diagnosis, there must be a significant difference between a child's tested cognitive (or intellectual) level and his tested educational-achievement level. A child can have intelligence scores or abilities in the gifted range and still be learning disabled, or he can be at an average or below-average cognitive level but not test at the same level in educational achievement.

Learning disabilities vary in severity and likely arise from a conjunction of several factors. The difficulty of explaining them is just one of the many ways they are frustrating. Some experts seek to relate learning disabilities to certain underlying neuropsychological processes. They identify learning disabilities as innate handicaps that interfere with a child's abilities to store, process, or produce information. (See Chapter 2 for a discussion of these functions in the developing brain.) This interference can create a gap between a student's true capacity and her day-to-day performance.

Learning disabilities can appear in reading, writing, mathematics, or in some combination. The most common learning disability involves reading. It was once called dyslexia, a word whose Greek roots denote problems with reading. The term used to indicate that one "sees things backward" since children with reading disabilities sometimes confuse similar letters, such as *b* and *d*, and words, such as "was" and "saw." To read, all young children have to figure out how letters change according to their orientation: even though a cup is still a cup when it is upside down, a *b* can become a *d* or a *p* or a *q* by being turned upside down or flipped. Every reader confuses the order of letters or numbers sometimes, but children with reading and spelling disabilities may have more than the usual trouble remembering letter sequences and orientations.

Consider the three mental functions involved in learning to read: storing, processing, and producing. You must store each letter's name and what it looks like. You must also store the sounds associated with each letter and the rules that indicate which sound is appropriate in certain situations. Think about reading the word "cider" letter by letter:

c   The first letter is a word that sounds like "see." The letter itself can stand for any of the following three sounds: /k/, as in "cat," "cow," and "cub"; /s/, as in "city," "cent," and "cycle"; or /ch/, as in "cello."

i   The second letter, which is pronounced "eye," denotes that sound in some words, such as "mine," but a totally different sound in other words, such as "kid."

d   This letter is the most straightforward, as it has only one sound, but it is not "dee," which is the name of the letter. A child has to remember that *d* stands only for the sound at the front of the syllable "dee."

e   Like *i* and the other vowels, *e* symbolizes at least two sounds. In this word, however, it actually sounds like ə.

r   Although an *r* typically has one sound, the *e* and *r* sound differently together from when they are separate.

Finally, after sorting through all these letter and sound combinations, the child must remember the other name for "apple juice." Most students learn this kind of letter–sound association either by some sort of linguistic osmosis or through a few good lessons from the teacher. For a student with a reading disability, each step is a separate lesson and often requires memory aids with lots of drill and practice.

You might spot some signs of a possible reading disability in the classroom. One example is a child's inability to listen to a story at length. Children who don't enjoy listening may have trouble reading aloud: they may need lots of help decoding and sounding out words, guess at or skip words, or be very reluctant to read aloud. Students who read aloud *too* steadily, not noticing errors or failing to change their tone of voice in accordance with the story, may not be processing the meaning of the words they speak. Most children stop moving their lips when they read silently to themselves a few months after they learn to read, especially when encouraged to do so; children with reading problems are more likely to be struggling to decode words and thus continue to move their lips. Such problems usually show up early and stick with a reader. They may be hard to perceive at first, and many children find strategies to mask or get around their early problems. The greater challenges in late elementary school, however, make reading difficulties more obvious and more troubling.

A learning disability is not like appendicitis, which is painful but can be treated with surgery. A learning disability does not get cured. It is a neurological condition that is part of the brain from birth. This is more significant than a learning difference. Everyone has a different learning style, and every child with a learning disability has strengths in other areas. But ten to fifteen percent of all learners have more than a learning difference; their education requires a different approach, and they will need to be taught different strategies for learning that they will rely on all their lives. Remember that a learning disability is a school-based problem with school-based solutions. With special educational help, a student with a learning disability can learn basic skills and acquire strategies for work that is more advanced.

It is the school's responsibility to determine which procedures will be successful and make them available to the students who need them.

Some students with learning disabilities may need special education throughout their school careers. Others may move on to junior high and high school needing only classroom modifications and course selections calibrated to match their strengths and weaknesses. A student may record her teachers' lectures rather than, or in addition to, taking notes. She may be drawn to drama as a way to express herself if writing is difficult. Many students with learning disabilities go on to higher education and careers. Nothing about a learning disability in and of itself limits a child's eventual career choice or potential for success.

Special Education Services

Identifying children who may have special needs should begin early so that families can take advantage of the special education services in their district as soon as possible to get the greatest benefits. These services are available through school systems and may be available to preschool children. Arranging for special school services for a child requires collaboration with other school staff and administrators and the child's parents or caregivers. When a student is having trouble with some aspect of learning, the school typically brings together a team to share impressions and thoughts on how to help her. This team includes you, her parents, and perhaps other school personnel: a reading specialist, speech and language pathologist, psychologist, and/or principal. Together you develop a plan to make accommodations for the child in your classroom. Such interventions might include extra small-group instruction in the problem area, increased home–school coordination, or a simple behavior-management system. Often these changes are enough to help a child make developmental progress.

If a child continues to have difficulties, however, a more formal meeting may determine whether she needs an Individualized Educational Plan (IEP) or special education. The team that assembles for this meeting has different names in different states but may be called a planning and placement team (PPT), an IEP team, or a child study team. Here, we'll call it a PPT, and it consists of the relevant school personnel—usually the classroom teacher, the principal, the school psychologist, and a special education teacher—and the child's parents. The members work together to determine what makes sense for each individual child. Although meetings with the PPT may include numerous experts, remember that the child's parents are also experts on their child.

The first step is usually a comprehensive evaluation of the child by the school psychologist. Timely and comprehensive testing is an effective way to determine the child's strengths and weaknesses. After the evaluation, the psychologist will present the results to the group. The assessment may include a classification of "learning disabled." Many parents may resist applying a label to their child, but a student cannot receive special educational services without a formal diagnosis. Teachers understand that each child is much more than a label. They get to know their students very well and learn their unique abilities as well as their disabilities. The government and schools need a way to designate the students who most need that help, but it remains a school-based label, not a measure of intelligence or potential. It indicates that a student's academic skills are not at the same level as his intellectual skills and that he might benefit from special educational interventions.

The range of interventions that might be part of a child's IEP includes special tutoring, counseling, occupational therapy, physical therapy, speech and language therapy, or placement in a special classroom or school. Most educators and parents work very hard to provide an appropriate program in the child's local school, but school districts also support private-school placements for children whose disabilities require highly specialized services. The school's initial IEP must spell out the specific goals of the plan and (if the child will remain in her regular classroom) how you as the teacher will modify the child's lessons, how much time she will spend each week in special education, and the personnel responsible for carrying out further steps. Once approved, this plan will be in place for the entire next school year unless you or the parents request a new PPT. If dissatisfied with a child's program, however, the parents or the teacher can request a new PPT to revise the IEP at any time. As a final step before beginning the IEP, it is often helpful for teachers, parents, and the student to meet so that everyone hears about the new expectations.

As your students gradually move into the larger world beyond their immediate families, you have fostered their learning and development and become better acquainted with their individual personalities. You have watched their motor, cognitive, and language skills emerge. As they become part of the larger community, they will build on the foundation you have so carefully nurtured during their preschool years.

Parents' Roles in Supporting Children with Learning Disabilities

A parent of a student with learning disabilities has two roles: as an education advocate and as a supporter. At first, most parents find being an advocate to be the most daunting. It requires talking about their child's vulnerabilities with a group of professionals, some of whom they may not know well. It requires knowledge of educational methods, rules and regulations, and specialized terms of the field.

Being an advocate can be challenging for parents, who are not involved in the day-to-day education of their children. Many children will work either one-on-one or in a small group with a paraeducator who is specifically trained to teach children with learning disabilities and who will use different methods and materials from those found in the regular classroom. Effective teaching of students with learning disabilities is both diagnostic and prescriptive. The paraeducator begins with the child's test profile and determines what methods have worked for other students with similar profiles. She then fine-tunes her instruction based on each student's daily performance. Progress occurs slowly and in spurts. Parents can support their children by celebrating the good times and encouraging them after setbacks.

As a student with a learning disability progresses through the grades, assistance often switches from instruction in the basic skills of reading or math to help with study skills and strategies. Children with disabilities have an ever-increasing array of technology supports available to them to not just accommodate but also help drive improvement.

Being an advocate means that parents should learn about the services available in their community. Almost every category of special need has a national organization with local chapters that sponsor parent support groups. Every state has a department of education with a special education resource center and staff, as well as a federally funded parent advocacy center that can help secure resources.

Over time, many parents learn to navigate the services and find that their role as a supporter is actually more challenging than that of an advocate, but it is also more important. Every student who has problems in school worries to some degree about his level of intelligence. These worries probably start before the PPT, even before anyone suspects a problem, as the child struggles with his earliest lessons. Students see the progress and abilities of other children and they notice their parents' disappointment about their own progress and grades, and this can affect their self-esteem. Sometimes a therapist can help a child with a learning disability recognize his self-worth and his own strengths.

Children with learning disabilities need their parents' help in recognizing their strengths and weaknesses. Although parents may be reluctant to address their child's weaknesses, without doing so, their child is less likely to believe them when they praise her strengths.

When parents read aloud to their child, they should choose books on his intellectual level and not his reading level. This maintains his interest and pleasure in reading and protects his self-esteem. For older students with reading problems, there are books that speak to the interests and emotions of adolescents while using simple vocabulary and sentence structure.

Parents may feel tempted to focus on the areas where their child seems to need the most work, but it is important that they avoid turning everything into a lesson. Gifts and activities outside of school should match the child's strengths and interests, as they should for any child.

A child who has overcome learning disabilities in areas that were difficult for her is better able to recognize her strengths and to know what she wishes to do when she is an adult. She is also able to overcome the inevitable difficulties that arise from trying new things. By advocating for and supporting their child, the PPT can help her develop appropriate learning strategies and maintain her self-esteem, and therefore develop skills for succeeding in whatever field she chooses.

WRAP IT UP

Even with the best preparation, the transition to school can be difficult for some children. As a preschool teacher, you can help your students transition to preschool while also preparing them for kindergarten, which is the beginning of a child's formal education. Many children suffer from separation anxiety, which can make it difficult for them to adjust to being in a classroom away from their parents. Your patience and consistent presence can help an anxious child feel comfortable being away from his family in the classroom.

It is important to involve families in the classroom so that you can maintain open communication, in case you or the child's family has any concerns. Classroom volunteers can also be an invaluable resource for the students in the class and for you as the teacher. Not only can they provide assistance in the classroom, but parents who are involved with their child's school become advocates for their own children and for the school as a whole.

Discipline in school involves teaching students to follow rules and act appropriately; it does not involve punishment and suspension. When behavior issues arise, it is important to try to understand the source of the problem and to keep parents informed.

Special education may be needed for students with developmental disabilities or learning disabilities. Identification of these students should occur as early as possible so that the student and the family fully understand the challenges the student may face and provide the supports they need to thrive in school. That way, the family can take advantage of special education services that will maximize school success.

CHAPTER 8

A Child's Inner World of Feelings

Teachers need to draw on patience, understanding, and self-reflection to help their students recognize and manage their emotions.

The word *emotion* comes from the Latin for "to move out, to stir up, excite," and an emotion is a strong feeling that, in response to some external excitement, springs up and registers in the brain without any purposeful mental effort. Emotions—love and hate, joy and sorrow, pride and shame, and so on—stir or activate a person and affect the person's interactions with others. Our emotions are the essence of our humanity. The ability to trust our feelings and to reflect upon them develops in the earliest years of life.

Emotions are a universal language. Across all cultures, people share the basic emotions of happiness or anger, surprise or sadness, and their faces reflect them in much the same way. Even infants can distinguish these basic emotional expressions and, well within their first six months, can match tone of voice to facial expression.

Recognizing emotions in others is the first and most basic step in how people interact with one another.

Recognizing that a face is happy, angry, or sad is just the beginning. We also need to understand the reasons behind the emotion. Our own experiences can affect our interpretation of the emotion we observe in another person. For example, if a man smiles warmly, one person might think he's simply being polite, another person might perceive personal interest, and yet another might think that he had just received good news.

Emotional life involves not only being able to recognize what emotions look like in other people but also knowing how they feel to you—in your gut, head, muscles, and skin. You know the physical sensations, such as the lightness or warmth of happiness. While you share these basic sensations with other people, your own experience also affects your feelings, allowing you to attribute meaning to them.

Feelings can be unruly, ambiguous, forceful, or dramatic. You can hide your feelings or bury them so completely that you don't even know what they are. It is far better, however, to recognize your feelings, whatever they are. Only then can you understand what has caused them and respond to them effectively. Indeed, only then can you appreciate how they are affected by the social world you live in and your sense of self.

Many times people speak of emotional and cognitive selves as being distinct from each other. In fact, the feeling self and the cognitive self are intimate companions. As the feeling self surges with emotion, the cognitive self tries to manage, or channel, that emotion in the most positive way. It may take mental effort to figure out what has given rise to a particular emotion and to find a way to manage it constructively. Similarly, only through cognitive skills can you understand and respond to the feelings of other people affected by your emotions. Being a responsible, feeling person involves learning to identify and express your emotional self effectively, choosing which feelings to share and with whom, and reconciling your own feelings with those of others.

Feelings and emotions can draw people together or pull them apart, but by mastering their emotions, different kinds of people live in peace in their families and in society. The social child is one who learns to recognize and manage his or her emotions and to develop them in friendships, in school relationships, as a member of a family with its culture and traditions, and finally as a moral person. In this chapter, we will discuss all these aspects of the social development of children.

Emotions in Infancy

When parents welcome their newborn child into their life and she responds according to her own personality, they also bring her into the social world. Throughout the various stages of childhood, parents build on this first loving relationship to help their child discover and deal with her emotional self, both at home and in the world.

First Feelings: The Newborn's Emotions

The act of being born thrusts a newborn baby into a completely new sensory environment. His early growth and development involve adapting physically, cognitively, and emotionally. Although babies do, indeed, progress similarly overall, each child responds in his own way and time to the sensory aspects of his surroundings. Physical stimuli such as bright lights and sharp sounds can be overwhelming for a newborn. Her body is also newly functioning, and physical experiences adults take for granted and may barely notice feel like a barrage of sensations that she cannot yet sort out or make sense of.

A newborn's emotions are rooted in these most basic body sensations. Happiness is being warm, full, and alert. It is being held comfortably and hearing someone singing a soothing melody. Unhappiness comes from being hungry, tired, cold, uncomfortable, startled by a loud noise, or alone with no one responding. The meanings of a very young infant's emotions derive from those physical experiences and her parents' responses. She comes to associate feeling cold and hungry with unhappiness, in part because those sensations feel unpleasant and then are relieved and in part because of her parents' response to her at the time. Hearing her parents put her emotions into words helps a baby build up a repertoire of meanings, good and bad, for her physical feelings.

As an infant gradually becomes used to the sensations of the outside world in his first months, he begins to express his tolerances and preferences. A baby's random and unpredictable behaviors start to fade. He will begin to develop predictable patterns of feeding and sleeping. The differences in a baby's cries become more easily recognizable, and caregivers learn how to respond, strengthening the meanings the baby gives to his sensations, thus validating his emotions and encouraging him to attend to them on his own.

Temperament and Personality

An adult's particular mode of behavior and reaction is usually referred to as his or her personality. It includes all of the abilities, habits, and preferences that a person develops through experience and learning and that make him or her different from other people. Since babies have little experience in life, however, we call their typical emotional and behavioral responses to the environment "temperament." Temperament likely has a genetic basis, while personality emerges through the interaction between genes and environment. Temperament may be thought of as the inherited personality traits—normal activity level or dominant mood, for instance—that become evident even in early childhood.

The most basic characteristic of temperament may be an infant's reaction to a new situation or challenge—in other words, the excitability of her central nervous system. Adults certainly vary in the degree to which stimulation excites them: that is, in terms of increases in heart rate, brain activity, sweating, and even motor behavior. Among infants, differences in physiological responsiveness seem to be mirrored in behavioral patterns. The ones who avoid the unfamiliar, act hesitantly, and are easily overwhelmed tend to cry more easily, be less active, and show less curiosity. When present, this trait, called "inhibition" by some researchers, often persists from infancy through early childhood and may be the most consistent or stable of the early temperament characteristics.

Parents generally believe in the stability and predictability of their child's personality, and some research suggests that early temperaments correlate to school-age behaviors. However, early temperament does not reliably predict later personality. For one thing, different patterns of temperament elicit different patterns of behavior and responses from parents, and experience is what shapes temperament into personality. An infant with unpredictable moods and slow adaptation to change is more stressful and tiring for parents than the adaptive, easy baby who needs (and elicits) a different style of parenting. She requires more predictable, consistent, steady responses from her parents, and they should be flexible and creative if she responds poorly or irritably to their caring. Since mothers and fathers bring their own personalities and beliefs to their parenting, some parents will feel anxious or guilty about their "difficult" baby, others will find him a challenge, and still others may feel inclined to give up and pull away. Different caregiving patterns may reinforce or mitigate the tendencies that make a baby challenging. So a baby's temperament is shaping his parents' behavior even as they are helping his personality to emerge.

The relationship between temperament and later personality is affected by a child's wider social environment. The value a culture ascribes to independence, exuberance, and curiosity shapes how people outside the family perceive and respond to a young child's behavior. In the United States, we tend to encourage these traits, but they have not always been rewarded in all children. Some societies find independence and curiosity to be alarming, and parents in those cultures may encourage more cautious behavior. Thus, despite its biological basis, a child's temperament changes constantly as a result of interactions between a child, her parents, and her experiences with the wider world. The fussy, irritable toddler actually may develop into a graceful, charming, flexible adolescent, while the easygoing baby may be anxious, depressed, and withdrawn as a teenager.

Socialization in Infancy

A baby comes into the world ready for the stimulation of social exchange. As he becomes used to life outside the womb, he becomes more attentive to his immediate surroundings. A newborn's eyes are capable of seeing objects at many distances, but in the first months his eye muscles are best suited for viewing objects that are eight to ten inches away from his face. This distance is just right for him to study his parents or caregivers as they hold him and talk to him. His favorite sights are faces, and he listens intently as they speak to him. Though he still cannot distinguish one person from another, he does notice social interaction, expressions, intonation, and attention. (See Chapter 5 for more on language.)

In time, interactions with caregivers will bring a smile to his face. This expression is a bid for a social response, which in turn makes both infant and caregiver feel pleasure. After many such moments of sharing smiles, an infant can draw his own individual meaning from the experience.

Social interaction of all kinds, from feeding to diapering to cuddling, leads a child to feel emotionally attached to the adults in her life. By three months or so, an infant can distinguish the adults who are special to her from other people. Week by week, her preferences for companionship become clearer. She will become most attached to the person or people who have invested the most time in keeping her company and loving her.

It is in these first relationships that a baby experiences the mixture of affection, disappointment, anger, frustration, and other intense feelings that constitute love. In a baby's first love relationship, he learns about himself, other people, and the world. This experience is the foundation for his learning about emotions and how to cope with them.

A baby's devotion to and loving feelings for his parents will remain prominent in his life for some time. In his second six months he can certainly include others in his love, but no one else will be as special as his parents are. He may begin to experience separation anxiety if his parents leave the room. An infant is aware of his parents' absence but cannot picture them in his mind or be confident that they will return. Some infants experience this more acutely than others. During the next twelve months, an infant learns through continual experience that things do not cease to exist just because he can no longer see them. And he will understand that, though his parents may leave his presence, they will return.

As a baby becomes accustomed to daily patterns, she begins to build up expectations that those patterns will continue. When a familiar routine takes an unexpected twist, she may become distressed and lose confidence, at least temporarily, in her understanding of the world. Any unexpected change in an established pattern can prompt a fearful reaction from an infant. Brand-new people or places may also produce fear. As in many other aspects of temperament (see also pages 123–124), children differ in their tolerance of intense and novel experiences, and they look to their parents to interpret the world for them. Parents let their infant know not only what they think is safe, but also which things are good or bad and which activities are fun or not fun.

During his first year of life, a baby develops in extraordinary ways, growing from a tiny newcomer into a toddler with strong desires and preferences that he can clearly demonstrate.

Through his attentiveness to faces and the loving care of a few special people, an infant forms his first love attachment. This bond arises out of an emotional dialogue that relies on expressiveness, responsiveness, and sharing feelings with one another, and he becomes skilled at reading the emotional reactions in faces and voices, and can tell whether he can safely proceed with his explorations. Although a one-year-old has usually discovered that people and things do not cease to exist if they are out of sight, he has yet to see his caregivers as being separate from him. Gaining an understanding of his own individuality is part of the next step in a child's emotional development.

Unsteady Balance: A Toddler's Emotional Life

The major developments that occur during the second year can make a toddler seem older than her years. Her emotional balance is delicate, however, and a small snag in whatever she is doing can upset it.

Toddlers are explorers. They investigate their surroundings endlessly, and are just as inquisitive about people. Up until about thirteen months, a child is most likely to be confused or upset when he sees someone in distress; he is unlikely to understand the other person's emotions. As a toddler, his understanding of others' emotions begins to develop, and he may try to comfort someone who is crying. He is beginning to appreciate that emotions have causes and to identify what makes people happy or sad. He is also beginning to recognize that other people's feelings are separate from his own: he can be happy while another person is sad.

Sometimes, a toddler explores the relationship between events and emotions by deliberately provoking a reaction. His curiosity is innocent and natural. He is unable to distinguish right from wrong, so he cannot understand the consequences of his actions or recall how he felt when something similar happened to him. He needs help to learn from his experiences and often needs repeated reminders.

A toddler's cognitive abilities are not fully formed. Though she may use a variety of words, she does not understand many subtleties. Her memory for some details and past events is selective and short. Since she has no capacity for forethought, she cannot anticipate the results of her behavior. Since she acts on what she is feeling in the moment, she can be impulsive. Dealing with these constantly changing feelings can be difficult for both a child and her caregivers.

Toddlers begin to learn that they are separate from their parents and caregivers and have different likes and dislikes. They seek autonomy yet still need protection and emotional support. Toddlers embrace the world with curiosity and find challenges and excitement everywhere. That beckoning world can also be dangerous, and eighteen months is the peak age for injuries because a toddler's curiosity and mobility often outpace her ability to judge danger.

A toddler's comprehension of the world is still limited, and he may feel apprehensive about new things he encounters as well as what appears in his thoughts and imagination. He may feel particularly apprehensive at bedtime, when he is about to be left alone, but consistency and routine can help with his worries. If his immediate surroundings are unchanging and predictable, the world will seem a little less uncertain and daunting.

Gathering information everywhere, a toddler is on a mission to understand her social as well as physical world. At the same time, she is deepening her investigations into other people's emotions and their causes. As she moves toward independence, her confidence in her understanding grows along with her ability to express her emotions. The increasing sophistication of these cognitive skills is one thing that separates a toddler from a young child.

Trying on Emotions: Early Childhood

As a child enters his third year, his playtime will take on some new qualities. He knows his own desires and beliefs and can identify them. His imitative play is supplanted by pure imaginative play (see Chapter 4), and his capacity for complex thought increases. He can, for example, hold an object in mind and think about it even when it is not present. With this ability, a child is able to enter into new and important learning realms, imagining fictional situations and identifying them as such.

Understanding another person's emotions means that a child must be able to imagine them. In her play, a child can pretend to want something another person wants. She examines that person's situation, imagining

her own desire being satisfied or frustrated. She can anticipate the emotion that is likely to arise in that person at either outcome and assign it to the person in her pretend scenario. Through this kind of pretend play, which can go on for hours, a child begins to be able to explain and predict other people's behavior and emotions in real life.

Imagination is powerful. At times, as a child immerses himself in different realms, he may hesitate on the edge of his understanding of the moment. He may need to check with you or his playmates to confirm that the situation is fictional. Sometimes the play can become too intense, creating real fear. If you acknowledge that a child's feelings at that moment are real and help him recognize what he is feeling, you make it easier for him to sort out the reality of the situation. Such a discussion helps him manage the experience, feel comfortable in his imagination and play, and trust the emotional support and anchor in reality his caregivers provide.

During their preschool years, children's fears become somewhat more realistic. The objects of their fear may be real (wolves, tigers, or sharks), but the likelihood of them actually having to face one of those fears is slim. This developmental shift reflects not only a child's increasing knowledge about the world but also his more sophisticated ability to fantasize about things he cannot see or understand.

Some children have strong, overwhelming worries and fears that are not simply responses to developmental pressures or the stresses of day-to-day life. These may grow significantly in response to a stressful life event—such as the birth of a new sibling, an illness, a death in the family, or a family move—and can interfere with a child's life at school and at home. Caregivers can feel completely helpless when a very young child is frightened and worried, and it can be difficult to appreciate the strength of a child's fear. Children need time to think through their most pressing worries and fears, and sometimes can work them out in their own ways with imaginative play (see Chapter 4). Thinking, playing, and talking can help, if the child's world is predictably and consistently secure, caring, and accepting.

As children become more proficient in understanding emotional expression, they also learn the difference between apparent and actual emotions. By age three or four, a child can hide her disappointment to a certain degree. Adults often coach their children to adopt social rules and polite behavior by, for example, prompting a youngster to smile and say thank you for a present she has received but is not terribly happy with. Although young children become quite able to modify their displays of emotion, they do so at this age simply to conform; they do not intend to mislead anyone.

They also do not expect that people might intentionally mislead one another, and they can easily be deceived or confused when a grown-up displays one emotion while concealing another. He often knows when something is bothering the people he loves—even his teacher. If you are having a bad day, a student may try to find out what's wrong. If you smile weakly in response and say that everything is fine, you give him a mixed message, confusing him. Having no idea why you would deny your feelings, he is no longer sure about what he saw. Consistently denying your feelings to a child can seriously impair his own ability to read his and others' emotions throughout his life. It is best to give him a simple, honest, understandable version of what is bothering you, framing your explanation in language and concepts that he can understand. Openly discussing your feelings and helping a child find words for his emotions will confirm his ability to perceive emotions and thereby enhance his understanding and self-confidence. (See "Self-Esteem and Why It Matters.")

Nonetheless, a three-year-old is now as skilled at reading body language as he was at reading faces when he was an infant.

Self-Esteem and Why It Matters

Self-esteem is a sense of inner pride in yourself as a feeling, effective person. This pride is not simply in outward success or competence; indeed, it may not reflect them at all. Some of the brightest and most successful individuals feel inadequate. Despite an outward appearance of self-assurance, privately they are convinced that they do not deserve their success and good fortune, and they are waiting to be found out as deficient and fake. Although their anxieties may have fueled their urge to achieve, they cannot truly judge or enjoy their success. This basic lack of self-esteem can cause emotional turmoil and interfere with a person's relationships with others.

A person's self-image, or how she feels about herself, has its roots in infancy and early childhood. It is based on the actions and words of her caregivers, including parents, teachers, nannies, grandparents, aunts, and uncles. When parents tell their baby how much they love her, how handsome, fast, quick, curious, or strong she is, they are beginning to build her self-image and, hence, her self-esteem. Similarly, if a parent notes only a child's misbehavior or comments only on what she cannot do well, she begins to see herself as a failure, which lowers her self-esteem. Young children sense their parents' doubts and anxieties. Parents who worry excessively that their child may not be able to throw a ball well enough to play Little League or may never do as well in school as her older brother also erode her self-esteem.

Parents reinforce their child's self-esteem when they let him know that they value him as an individual, whatever his strengths and weaknesses. He may not run fast enough to make the track team, but they love and respect him for trying. She may have trouble reading, but they trust her judgment and admire her sense of humor. It is important for parents and caregivers alike not to teach a child to accept lowered standards or to smother him with empty praise. Rather, they should help him value himself for what he does well, try hard, and accept what he cannot do as well as others.

As children get older, they naturally compare themselves with their peers. That urge is especially strong in adolescence, when children, buffeted by physical changes in their bodies and new questions of identity outside the family, have more difficulty feeling good about themselves. With this loss of self-esteem, they tend to listen to the judgment of other people, rather than their own. Self-esteem can be a child's internal compass where moral values, goals, and desires are concerned, and can protect against peer pressure and other external pressures. A child who feels good about himself believes that it is important to do what gives him satisfaction. And, if his caregivers have helped him develop a moral grounding, he will be most satisfied when he behaves well.

Children who feel strong, competent, secure, and adaptable and who understand themselves are able to weather the ups and downs of life far more easily than those who don't have high self-esteem. They are also better able to take pleasure in others' successes. These feelings are not luxuries: they are fundamental to functioning fully and successfully as a human being.

A Widening Emotional Life: The School-Age Child

By the time a child is ready for elementary school, more mental and physical transformations have shaped her emotional responses. Adults can reason and bargain with her, and she can do much more for herself. Her memory capacity has increased; she now has hindsight and foresight, so can remember and wait and look forward to what is coming. Her language skills and their associated cognitive abilities are at a crucial point in their development. She is no longer using language simply to label objects. She is now able to tell stories, to think about how things and people go together, to place events in the past and wishes in the future. She knows that her thoughts are her own and that other people have their own worlds of thoughts and feelings.

Each growth spurt and every new experience triggers both new and familiar feelings. Some feelings will confuse him, whereas others will be stressful or simply unfamiliar. Each situation evoking these feelings will be occasions for him to reflect on his inner world and to develop language that will help him understand these kinds of feelings. The more a child is able to bring his cognitive self to bear on his inner world, the more effective and confident he will be.

A school-age child's increasing cognitive abilities also allow her to see and empathize with another person's outlook, rather than projecting her own emotional responses onto that person. She can remain somewhat detached, knowing that a situation does not directly involve her, or she can choose to respond. She gains more awareness of her own feelings and comes to appreciate that actions that cause distress to others are wrong. As children attempt to refine their social skills, they become more conscious of which behaviors do and do not earn approval from adults. In the early part of this stage, a child longs for adult approval and will often try hard to behave like a grown-up. He will mimic adult body language and consciously try to refine his own behavior to match his understanding of what he sees. His games and pretend play will aid his social learning and help him emotionally process his own experiences and those he may have heard about, witnessed, or simply imagined. (See Chapter 4 for more about play.)

With the maturing cognitive abilities of school-age children, fears begin to involve plausible situations such as struggling in school or not making a sports team. Adults can relate to worries about being accepted, fitting in, and measuring up, so you may find it easier to talk to older children about their realistic worries, rather than trying to rationalize with a toddler who is convinced a dinosaur will come into her room at night. Despite being able to talk about their fears more than young children, older children can also mask those fears with aggressive behavior toward classmates. Anxieties over home situations can affect behavior in school and vice versa, so if you observe aggression in a student, you might consider what anxieties that student might be facing at home.

Controlling Emotional Expression

Learning that actions have consequences is a big step toward learning how to manage emotions.

The new experience of being in school and interacting with other children and adults transforms a child's consciousness about people, and he becomes very interested in social relationships outside the family. Now he can appreciate how people interact and that their actions have consequences. He realizes that his own actions do as well. To act on this realization, he needs to learn how to control the way he expresses his emotions.

Starting at about age four, children sense that their very intense feelings will wane in strength over time. That knowledge helps them learn, by about age six, that they can actually manage their emotions, and they see that the strength of an emotion is connected with how much they continue to think about its cause. If a child wants to stop feeling sad, he might try to distract himself so as to push away thoughts about what caused his sadness. He learns that choosing to do something that he knows will make him happy can change his mood. He may ask for help, or talk with you about feeling bad, or make up a pretend story. At this age, children can develop a repertoire of ways to cope with and understand their feelings.

You can encourage your students' interest in practicing socially acceptable behavior by teaching them the rules and conventions for displaying emotion publicly. For example, you can teach them not to brag when they win a competition because it makes their peers feel bad. Children around this age learn to understand and respect another person's feelings as well as their own. A child can realize that there are public and private feelings and that some social situations may require her to keep some feelings to herself and share them later with friends and relatives.

With a child's recognition of her private emotional world, she begins to appreciate its potential. With her new ability to be introspective and to identify her own emotions, she can take a step back and look at herself as if she were an observer. The ability to hold two or more views of herself allows her to decide which picture she would like to display outwardly. In different situations, she may choose to conceal her true response, either to protect her own feelings from the reaction of observers or to protect an observer's feelings. She also learns that the way she exhibits emotions can mislead other people.

The fact that children should learn to limit their display of emotion in certain social situations doesn't mean, of course, that they have to limit their usual feelings. Feelings are internal and unwilled; emotional displays are external and subject to control. Cultures and families differ greatly in how much emotion they consider acceptable for people to exhibit. In some houses, children hear their parents and other relatives laugh loudly, cry easily, and raise their voices in everyday conversation without implying any anger. In others, children grow up learning to keep their feelings to themselves. Children in both kinds of households have strong feelings, even as they learn to manage them according to their environment and temperament. Traditionally, American culture has had different expectations for the emotional expression of boys and girls, discouraging boys from showing their vulnerability and girls from being competitive. The most important message has been the same for all: while it isn't always easy to learn when it is appropriate to display emotions or how to do so, a child's strong feelings are central to his or her life and should be recognized and respected.

Internalizing Responsibility

Over the next few years, as a child comes to feel responsible for some of his own successes, challenges, and mistakes, he begins to understand such social emotions as pride, shame, and guilt. Younger children can experience pride based upon the approval of other people, but they have not yet developed their own standards or their own sense of satisfaction at behaving in a way they feel good about. At around eight years old, children begin to observe and judge their own actions according to what they believe another person's reaction would be. This internalization means that the child has incorporated into her own mental world the responses of her parents and other important adults and is a signal that she has begun to acknowledge some degree of personal responsibility. Now, no longer needing solely to look to others for judgment, she can look inside herself.

Aggressiveness and Anger

Aggressiveness and anger are typically thought of as negative emotions that go hand in hand: you are angry when you have been injured or wronged and thus feel aggressive toward the cause of that injury. Aggressiveness is not, however, always related to anger. Sometimes you are aggressive in order to gain what you believe to be rightfully yours. Of course, if the other party disagrees with your sense of ownership, anger soon erupts. Many a playground scuffle begins with one child claiming sole right to the sandbox. Aggressiveness is also not always destructive; indeed, it is the core of one's being necessarily and adaptively assertive, which can serve important social roles. American culture often encourages young people to be able to stand up for themselves, to take action against things that upset them, and to mobilize their energies to attain high ambitions. Yet this same culture also wants children to manage their feelings, to play fair, and to love each other. How to instill that balance in a child is a challenge to many caregivers.

Aggressive behavior in young children has many roots. While some factors in a child's aggression, such as her basic tolerance for frustration, seem to depend in large part on genes, many others are shaped by what she learns from her experiences with parents and teachers. At the very least, aggressive behavior always expresses particular needs and feelings, whether in a child who is extremely anxious on the first day of school or in another who is tired and overwhelmed. A two-year-old who has only acquired a few words may be more aggressive than his peers because he has no other means to express either his needs or his frustrations. If you can interpret a child's behavior in this light, especially when he is young, you will be better able to help him express his frustration positively without hurting anyone else.

Some children rarely, if ever, express themselves through aggressive behavior, while others are comfortable doing so. Not all thoughts or fantasies lead to aggressive behavior, and not all aggressive behavior is motivated by willful, hateful, or destructive feelings. In infants, aggression is mostly the expression of a need that is not quite satisfied. At first, when a baby is frustrated—by, say, not being able to reach a toy that she wants—she expresses herself by crying inconsolably. As she gets a bit older, she might push a parent away, hit, or throw something. Infants usually do not mean to harm people or things, nor do they even realize they have the power to do so, but they can tell when you are upset by their behavior.

For very young children eager for freedom, aggressive behavior can express independence. Through this aggressive behavior, a child can assert his own space and place in the world or a toddler can express his desire for control. This desire is often in conflict with a toddler's feeling of being small, dependent, and powerless. Developmentally, it is no accident that temper tantrums begin as children start to experiment with separation from their parents. The more they move away, the more dependent and little they feel.

Aggressive behavior in preschool children has different intents, causes, and outcomes. (See "Eric and His Dinosaur," on the next page.) In trying to figure out why a child is biting or hitting, ask where she directs her violence: toward other people or only toward inanimate objects? In other words, does she kick and break toys or kick and hurt her classmates, siblings, and parents? What typically starts the aggressive behavior? Is she frustrated because she wants a toy she cannot have or because she wants to be hugged by a busy parent or teacher?

Aggressive behavior is not always tied to anger, so determining the reason a child is acting aggressively can be a challenging task for a preschool teacher.

Eric and His Dinosaur

For Eric, a four-year-old boy, play was very exciting. He was fond of pretending to be a strong, invincible character encountering ferocious dinosaurs. Eric was often active, even wild, in this game. But the dinosaurs never seemed to be vanquished. They always returned, even more frightening than before. When Eric was deepest in this play, he would jump at the slightest unexpected sound and anxiously ask his teacher, "What's that?" Sometimes he would say with fearful certainty, "The dinosaurs are coming."

Eric was well liked by his teachers and the other children at his preschool. His teachers appreciated his verbal skills and vivid imagination but found his behavior extremely difficult to manage. He was especially disruptive on days when the class's schedule or usual activities did not go as planned. Sometimes, for no apparent reason, Eric would push or even hit another child. At these moments, even his calmest, firmest teacher had trouble helping him settle down. The preschool staff was worried about how Eric was going to do in a larger, more stimulating kindergarten classroom.

As spring came around, they met with Eric's parents and suggested that, despite his obvious intelligence, he was not ready to start school. He was still developing the ability to cope with changes to his routines and to manage his own frightening thoughts. And so Eric spent another year at the preschool, a familiar place he knew and liked. He still played exuberantly, but one day he announced to his teacher that he had tamed the dinosaur: "It's my friend now." Gradually his overall behavior grew calmer. The next September, Eric was ready to enter kindergarten and did very well.

Is she very tired or very excited? Is she reacting to another child's teasing? Did another child hit or push her? Consider the apparent intent of a child's aggressive behavior. Is it a means to an end—to get the desired toy or sit on your lap? Is it to create a personal space? Does the goal seem to be to injure or destroy or is it really to gain another person's attention, win in a game, or get the best seat in circle time? No child acts aggressively in the same way with the same reasons in every situation. But if you identify what a child really wants, you can tell her not to push or hit while showing her a better way to achieve her aim. Thus, you reduce her frustration and her need to act out.

When evaluating a child's aggression, consider how it might be linked to his fears and worries. His behavior may be a way for him to express, without acting fearful, that he is really worried deep down. Although not all aggressive feelings in children reflect deep-seated fears and anxiety, parents and teachers need to be aware of this possibility. In addition, aggressive thoughts worry young children. That anxiety might, in turn, encourage a child to be even more bold and aggressive.

Remember also that there is little to no separation between thoughts and action in the minds of children younger than four or five. If by coincidence, a child's thought seems to come true—for example, a three-year-old pretending to be a pirate may declare that he has killed everyone, and by chance, his mother comes home from work late that evening—he may start to wonder whether he has actually done what he has imagined. Young children also suspect that other people know exactly what they are thinking, including their desires for power and triumph. A child may, therefore, half-expect adults to punish her for her aggressive thoughts, even if she never acts on them.

Physically aggressive behavior—hitting, biting, pushing, kicking—begins to subside by the time most children reach their third or, at the latest, their fourth birthday. Verbal aggression, on the other hand—shouting, yelling, and name-calling—increases between the ages of two and four as children gain more language skills. Most often, all kinds of hostile behavior, whether verbal or physical, diminish in frequency by the time children are five or six and entering the first and second grades.

Learning to handle both positive and negative emotions is difficult for children; indeed, some adults still struggle with it. Your behavior toward a child will teach her that every human being has feelings—that they love the most important people in their lives for who they are, yet at the same time may get mad at their quirks and disappointing qualities. This knowledge, acquired early in life, will undergird all of a child's relationships with other people. It is the framework for the social tasks ahead, including that most important one of developing a conscience and becoming a moral person.

Infants learn to recognize emotions in the faces of their caregivers, and as they develop, they learn to understand the causes of certain emotions. Their own emotions come from their basic body sensations, and they gradually develop tolerances and preferences. Their responses to these emotions and their environment influence their temperament and personality. Through socialization, infants develop emotional attachment, which can lead to separation anxiety. They also learn daily patterns and feel secure in their predictability.

Toddlers begin to understand others' emotions and their causes. They may try to influence those emotions by comforting someone who is upset or provoking a reaction out of someone. They learn that they are separate from parents and caregivers but still need protection, so they are curious and independent sometimes and need the comfort of a caregiver at other times.

Preschool-age children are strongly influenced by imagination. They are able to imagine others' emotions or to predict others' responses, and they often use and further develop their understanding of emotion during pretend play. Preschool children learn to suppress emotions to follow social rules, but they do not intend to mislead anyone. They can interpret others' feelings based on body language and may try to help a loved one feel better.

The increasing cognitive abilities of a school-age child allow them to interpret their own and others' complex emotions. Their language skills allow them to communicate their own feelings and those of others. They begin to link an action with its consequences. They also learn that, since feelings can weaken over time, distraction can help improve their mood. At this age, children also learn the accepted ways of displaying emotion publicly and being sensitive to others' feelings.

Aggressiveness is not limited to a particular age range, nor always related to anger. Younger children may be more likely to display aggressiveness because it is often related to frustration, and that frustration may have a variety of causes. Determining the cause for the frustration may help resolve the aggression. Managing these negative as well as positive emotions is challenging for children, but it is an important skill for them to learn to help them develop healthy relationships throughout their lives.

CHAPTER 9

Friends: A Child's Expanding Social World

When you see preschool children form friendships, you are observing one of the most intense and significant aspects of being a child.

Playing with friends is one of the best parts of childhood. Your own memories from childhood may be full of moments with friends. Friendship is one of the most intense, pleasurable, and significant aspects of being a child, and childhood friendships form the foundation for other close social interactions. They are the practice ground for dealing with all the emotions of interpersonal relationships. As such, friendships are also a potential source of trouble, in part because children are just learning to handle their emotions.

A child's capacity for friendship has its roots in his relationships with his parents and caregivers. In many ways, these adults become his first friends as they interact, communicate, and play simple games with him in the first weeks and months of his life. If these interactions are not open and happy, a child is more likely to have trouble interpreting other people's wishes and emotional cues as he gets older. Parents are, however, much more than friends to their infant. The child quickly comes to see them as the provider of everything she needs to live, and they are both protectors and disciplinarians. As part of her healthy development, she will begin to form friendships with peers. These relationships will be on a more equal footing than the ones with her parents, who have dedicated themselves to always loving and caring for her.

If a child has an older sibling or a twin, his first true friendship is most likely to be with that brother or sister. A sibling relationship usually contains a mix of feelings: love, loyalty, pride, jealousy, and rivalry, to name a few. It differs from later friendships because the connection between children is involuntary. They share toys and games because they are in the same household, and, while they can stop playing together, they cannot go far apart. Nevertheless, the early experience of being close to a brother or sister is a major influence on a child's relationships with other children.

Young children often find their first friends within their family, but as they get older, they find friends in the neighborhood or in their school.

As she grows up, she will respond to qualities in others that, consciously or unconsciously, remind her of her siblings, or she will seek companions who intrigue her for being different from the people she knows at home.

For an only child, sometimes a cousin is a first friend, and their cousin relationship may resemble that of siblings. If the only child has no young family members nearby, parents may look in their own social circles, their neighborhood, or the child's school to find potential playmates for her. You may observe these important early friendships form in your classroom.

Do not be surprised when you observe moments of friction between young children during the school day. Playing with other children is a social skill that young children learn over time, and it contributes to the social development of both the child and her playmates. As you watch a child playing with her friends, you may also notice some aspects of her personality you have not had the chance to see before: her ability (or inability) to share toys and precious possessions, her insistence on certain prized roles in pretending, or the ease with which she includes new playmates in her games. In this chapter, we discuss how children make friends in the preschool and school years and how to deal with the problems that may arise from these relationships.

The Preschool Years

In the preschool years, children learn about relationships with persons other than their parents and their close family. A four-year-old's friends may change from week to week, or she might declare that her cat or a girl she has created in her mind is her friend (see "Imaginary Friends"). A preschooler's friendships will often be turbulent and unpredictable. In these early friendships, children not only enjoy the comfort of having playmates but also learn how to deal with the difficult emotions of feeling rejection or anger.

Friends and Companions

Developmental experts once suggested that preschool children are merely companions or play partners for each other. Real friendship comes later, they said, during elementary school. This perspective has changed because children these days have many more opportunities to develop close relationships with their young peers in preschool or day care. These friendships may wither in a short time, then blossom again. These short-lived friendships may seem too shallow to be called friendships at all, but each relationship is important to a child as he learns about the world.

A young child usually has an idea of what a "friend" is; the word is in his vocabulary, and he uses it early. He may relate to other children as a partner in play, a trusted companion, or an ally in overcoming obstacles. Some children in day care or preschool find security in choosing a particular friend as an anchor within the group. When one child's need for such companionship becomes extreme, she may not be able to function when her chosen friend is absent. The pair may exclude others from their play. Although this behavior may constitute dependency rather than friendship, finding security in a new relationship is one way for a child to adapt to separation from home and to form bonds with others.

In preschool, children interact with many of the other students in the class each day. They move in and out of different areas and forms of play. A well-planned schedule includes activities for small groups, large groups, and individuals. Sometimes an activity determines which, and how many, children can participate. Teachers may pair children or create groups for various projects,

Children as young as three might save a seat for a classmate or ask the same classmate to play a game every day, demonstrating a capacity for real friendship at a very young age.

Imaginary Friends

As part of their overall imaginary play (see Chapter 4), many preschool children—up to half, according to some surveys—create imaginary companions and insist on their reality. Families often have to pretend to accommodate these invisible creatures, and parents may be conflicted about it. Some parents simply are not comfortable stepping inside their child's fantasies or may worry that playing along with their child will impede her from learning what is real. But invisible friends should not be a big concern for parents or teachers of preschoolers. In fact, they can serve an important role in a child's development. For children under five, the boundary between fact and fantasy is almost always hazy; in a few years, it will naturally grow clearer. If pressed, most preschoolers would agree that their friends are not really visible, not really hungry, not really sleeping beside them, but they would much prefer that you play along.

An imaginary playmate often provides a child with companionship when he is alone. Invisible friends interact with their creators, tease and are teased, instigate projects or follow along admiringly. A child's imaginary playmate usually has a name, a personality, and a gender that correspond with a child's wishes and even has a life-defining story. Unseen companions tend to maintain these core characteristics; even if, from month to month, a child adds details, his invisible friend's basic features and "history" remain the same, just as those of his real friends do.

Although it isn't always possible to trace the process by which an imaginary friend comes into a child's life, the forms that an imaginary friend takes often reflect a child's concerns and anxieties, as do her games. When a child is worried, her imaginary friend can offer her some psychological protection from her worries by taking on magical powers or even by succumbing to dangers in her place.

At times, a child may use an unseen companion as an alibi and blame that companion for something the child did. For other children, the invisible friend can constitute an extra conscience, even scolding as adults do. A child can create an air of secrecy when he decides the companion is lost or hiding. And all of the characteristics and actions of his invisible friend are unknown unless the child "translates."

Indeed, one of the biggest attractions of an imaginary friend is that it is a part of a preschooler's existence that she, and only she, can control. For this reason, wait until a child has invited you to interact with her invisible playmate. Deep down, she knows her friend is not real, and she might be quite disquieted if you take the lead in acting otherwise.

Children can create imaginary companions by assigning personalities to a stuffed toy. They may use different modes of speech to express individual desires, or every toy might speak in the same voice. If you want to play along, help your student explore different emotions and personality traits through stuffed animals. Improvise scripts about them and take heart from the fact that talking to a stuffed animal will be easier than talking to an imaginary companion. At least you can see when the child's pretend friend is in the room!

and at certain times of the day, each child should also have some choice about how he plays—alone or with others. Young children find pleasure in play with other children and discover the ability to be willing partners in a variety of games and activities.

Remember, a child's ability in this area is intertwined with the other skills and traits she is developing. So, for example, speech is important to friendship. If a child can communicate her ideas, she can share play space and equipment with a friend. Her friends, in turn, help her build her language skills. (See Chapter 5 for more on language.) And her ability to symbolize—to use blocks, for example, to represent roads and highways and to share this representation coherently—is the foundation for cooperative work in the later preschool years and the early years of elementary school.

In the preschool years, a child moves from solitary play through parallel (side by side) play to associative play. Cooperative play, the fond wish of parents and teachers, is sometimes within reach of older preschoolers and kindergartners, although the child developmentalist Jean Piaget held that truly cooperative play develops only at seven or eight years of age. This accomplishment depends, in part, on whether a child's environment at home or school fosters and encourages it. We know that games with firm rules and clear winners or losers are often not suitable for children under seven. In many ways, cooperative play emerges only when children are mature enough to tolerate a certain amount of competition.

When Preschool Friendships Become Worrisome

Strong—and sometimes intractable—feelings will suffuse preschoolers' play. Caregivers may hear heated arguments about who will assume what role in games. As some children learn to see the world through other people's eyes, there is bound to be friction between playmates. At whatever age, two children are unlikely to be precisely matched in thinking ability, temperament, and strength. And even if they were, they might see themselves as rivals rather than playmates. Also, children who are used to the company of adults may find their peers frustrating.

It is normal for any child to experience occasional difficulties in play that result in quarrels over roles or toys or attention (see "Tattling"). For the most part, these are situational difficulties to which you can find a practical solution. For example, a child may be trying to become part of an already established—and heretofore exclusive—twosome. In this case, you can suggest a toy with which he can either join the pair's play or start his own game with other children. When a child has persistent difficulties in playing with others, however, parents and teachers may become concerned. Such trouble might be rooted in various feelings. A child may be acting too bossy or stubborn, not showing the flexibility and humor that he needs to adapt to others. He may not like the fantasy games others choose, perhaps because he is being overly literal and is unable to pretend, because he finds fantasy threatening, or because he refuses to join in his friends' imaginary worlds. Sometimes a child's ideas are too complex for his peers, and he simply prefers to play alone or with an adult.

Even in the preschool setting, you may notice that two particular playmates have a negative influence on each other. If either of the children has spontaneously voiced any anxiety or regret about the friendship, you may want to raise the issue with the child's parents and steer each child to play with someone else for a while. If you choose to talk with the other child's parents as well, describe what you have

TATTLING

Tattling is a difficult issue, even for adults in their own lives as well as when dealing with children's relationships. When one child comes running to complain that another is breaking rules, adults feel conflicted. You do not want to get in the middle of every dispute between classmates and hope the children will learn to work out minor conflicts on their own. And you don't want a child to become known among his peers as a tattletale.

You should understand the different reasons a child might have for telling on others. Children are very sensitive to infractions of rules, and a child may tattle to diminish her anxiety at seeing another child doing or getting away with something she thinks is wrong or unsafe. But children may also tattle to gain favor with adults, to exact revenge on a sibling or classmate, or to take heat off themselves. This possible mix of heartfelt, noble, and devious motivations makes tattling complex.

When a young child runs to you accusing a classmate of hitting or taking a toy, what looks like tattling may also be asking for help. If these complaints arise several times in a day, you can help the complaining child develop strategies for dealing with what has upset him. You can remind him to use his words and say no. You can help him learn how to take turns sharing toys or to offer his playmate another toy as a compromise in a struggle. With thought, you can steer a younger child away from tattling and toward learning how to mediate aggression and play cooperatively.

Older children may have any of the same motives to tattle as younger ones. Yet, because of their close identification with peers, tattling is far more complex. On one hand, the greater independence of school-age children means that they can cause and get into much more trouble than can preschoolers tussling over a toy, yet school-age children can feel pressure not to tell adults about others' bad behavior. Older children need to learn when it is appropriate to bring adults into a situation and when they can handle it on their own.

There are, of course, situations in which an adult should interfere. If a child is being physically bullied or sees another child being mistreated, it is important not only to talk out the situation but to take steps to stop it. Talking over situations with a child as they arise may clarify the moral issues for both of you.

seen without being judgmental. Presenting the problem as a clash of personalities that you and the parents together can easily manage will be more effective.

If, however, both children are content with the relationship you find worrisome, consider why they may be drawn to each other. Sometimes a shy youngster feels stronger when teaming up with a more active, assertive playmate. A preschooler may be enjoying the chance to be silly or loud—a way of trying on roles, a constant activity at this age. You can remind them of your expectations of their behavior in school without

separating them, but this may not be enough. It may be necessary to watch the pair of friends more closely. Step in when things seem to be getting out of hand, and enforce the rules you have established in your classroom. If the children's behavior becomes dangerous or psychologically destructive, you should address the problem with the parents or caregivers of both children.

In most child-filled neighborhoods and in school, youngsters from two to five naturally play with others of different genders and with those who are close in age. Only when there are more years and wider developmental differences between children should you be concerned about a child's preference for playmates of a different age.

When children are young, parents usually schedule their playdates and other social activities and may worry about their children's popularity. However, overscheduling a child's time may affect her development or mood. When a child is in preschool or day care for much of the day, she needs some opportunity to play alone or with family members. She is probably not worrying about friendships in the same way her parents are. Sometimes parents project their own hopes for popularity—or worries about being rejected—onto their children and may want to know how their child plays in school. You can remind them that each person has his or her own level of need for companionship and solitude.

School-Age Children

In the school years, most children progress along the road to greater independence from their parents. Friendships developed during these years may be lifelong and are able to weather far better the emotional storms of anger and hurt. School-age children also learn about sharing friends with others, working in groups of friends, and even competing to be another child's best friend.

School-age friendships tend to have a more solid foundation and can survive disagreements better than those of preschool-aged children.

The Best of Friends

A first grader is away from home for most of the day, perhaps for all of it if he goes to after-school day care. He thus shares most of his experiences not with his parents and siblings, but with his peers in school. During these early school years, his sense of himself largely develops in reaction to, and against the backdrop of, his social group. He learns how to handle strong feelings in resolving conflicts with other children and develops new physical skills based on what his peers value and how much he wants to be like them.

A school-age child's move away from parents and other adult authority figures does not happen all at once. Six- and seven-year-olds still feel strongly dependent on their parents, but they look to slightly older children as they move into child society. Even as a child is striving for greater independence, her wish is not to take on adult responsibilities but, rather, to immerse herself in childhood and its subculture. This often starts with the children in her neighborhood and then switches to the children in her classes at school.

Toward the later elementary-school grades, a child's affiliation tends to become even more specific, and he allies himself with one or more friends in his classes who share his interests or traits. For most children, the term "best friend" designates not one particular boon companion but a quality of relationship; a child may have a whole group of "best friends" that he fervently values. Children at this age often form clubs or groups. Among school-age children, inclusion and rejection are more personal than they were in early childhood. Being excluded can be painful because defining oneself as belonging to a particular group is so important in these years.

This need to define a group is one reason popular culture—television shows, pop music, books, video games, and the latest toys—is so much a part of children's interactions at this age. These shared references are another way to confirm what the members of the group have in common. Sometimes groups of friends actually form because of such interests, but just as often the preferences of a group's leaders influence the interests of other children.

Defining groups is crucial to the way most school-age children develop a sense of the larger world and their place in it. Family provides a child a basic sense of who she is as a person. As she grows, that sense expands to include her place in her neighborhood, her school, and her country. Children go on to learn other forms of identity and ways of belonging, such as religious affiliation and ethnic and national origin. With their interest in formulating rules about how people behave, school-age children are prone to stereotyping, yet are able to appreciate when their parents teach them to look beyond surface characteristics to find qualities everyone shares.

Groups and their rules are central to the way school-age children play, but school-age children do not lose a sense of their own minds. As a child progresses through the middle years of childhood, she becomes more able to assert her will with peers and to accept not getting her own way. She has started to internalize a sense of right and wrong and can call on it when she disagrees with the choices others in her group are making.

In early adolescence, friendships often become more intimate and supportive, and less competitive. They are more individual, rather than based on a whole group. With tight friendships, children may feel less dependent on the larger group but can still enjoy being part of it. Their increasingly dependable friendships may help them feel secure enough to face the changes ahead. Finding and adjusting the balance between enjoying individual friendships and being an enthusiastic group participant is a constant throughout this stage of childhood.

Problems Making Friends, Problems with Friends

A child's move into the social world outside the family may be rocky. To form a comfortable relationship, two or more people must be able to interpret the many signals, nonverbal as well as verbal, that humans use to communicate. Individual children differ in the ability to "read" other people. Timidity in venturing forth, a need for continued parental approval, or feelings of insecurity can make it difficult to join the company of other children, and some young children feel more dependent on their home and family. If a child has not developed the skills his peers value, he may be embarrassed and worry about being teased.

If a child says that he does not have any friends, it may not mean that he is having serious difficulties. Few youngsters have immediate confidence in their relationships with others. A child's sadness may represent his feelings only today or this week. The fact that he is able to express his feelings is a sign that he understands the value of friendship.

If a child describes a conflict, a power struggle, or a feeling that another child has replaced him as someone's special friend, a trusted adult can offer him ways to help him find the motivation and the energy to try again after a frustrating day. All relationships have ups and downs, but children need time to experience this reality.

Some parents become concerned if their child does not seem to have a large group of friends, as her peers do. There are usually several children in every class who like to hang out with one close friend to the exclusion of all others. This may occur when two children do not share the predominant interest or tastes of their peers, or it may simply represent an earlier maturity and independence from peer pressures. Associating with peer groups before finding a particularly close friend is not a universal sequence, and each child approaches friendship in a slightly different way.

A child with few, rather than many, friends is quite different from a child who truly is an outsider, a loner. There may be concerns that indicate a need for consultation outside family and school, but these patterns of friendships and behavior may be relatively normal and understandable in the light of specific circumstances.

Even as a child moves into greater freedom, parents and caregivers continue to play a dominant role in her social life, supervising activities or ensuring they know where she is at all times. Children test rules about health, safety, and behavior and compare the rules imposed on them with the experiences of their friends. Often these complaints are simple pushes for independence. Occasionally, however, they may reflect the rebellious urgings of a child's friend or friends and can be cause for worry. Luckily, with older children, there is more opportunity for a parent to have a dialogue to express why some friendships are healthy and ask questions about others, especially those that involve risky or dangerous behavior.

A child's friendships are part of her life now and will be forever. With true friends, a child should be able to be her truest self, unburdened by worries about the need to belong, to compete, to achieve, or to pretend. Some close relationships born in childhood may last a lifetime, and close friends may become one's "relatives of choice." But even when childhood friends move or drift apart, the images of those relationships remain part of a child's identity.

WRAP IT UP

Friendships begin with family; a child's parents are often her first friends. As the parents move into a role more of protectors and disciplinarians, children begin to form friendships with siblings and then peers. Learning to play with other children is an important part of social development.

During the preschool years, friendships change frequently. Children may form a bond and become close friends, or they might gravitate to a different companion weekly. Planned activities in a preschool classroom allow for children to interact and play with other students in the class, while free play time allows them to choose the activities and friends. As young children develop their friendships, the relationships may have their challenges, such as arguments over toys or misunderstandings about feelings. Reinforcing classroom rules is often enough to resolve the disagreements.

Except for the rare preschool friendship, most lifelong friendships are formed during the school years. As children spend more time with peers, they develop connections with children who share their interests. School-age children often form groups based on interest or culture, which can reinforce a feeling of belonging for those in the group and can be painful for those who are excluded. Friendships may not always be easy, and some children may find it difficult to form strong friendships. However, parents and caregivers can help children navigate the ups and downs of friendships.

CHAPTER 10

Children's Mental Health

You have firsthand experience with the fact that no two children are alike, and all children develop differently. How, then, do you identify if one child's differences warrant extra attention?

Most parents expect that their child will be healthy all through childhood. But such a child is rare. Just as a child will have colds, growing pains, accidents, and other physical problems, so too will he have emotional or behavioral ones: some mild and transient, some painful, even frightening. A child's mental disturbance may be difficult for parents and families to accept or understand.

A child's mind and body are complex, so there are bound to be small, and sometimes large, glitches in the way they work: in the basic equipment, in the hardwiring of circuits in the brain, in the programming and development of behavior during the first years of life. Likewise, there will be outside events in the child's life that can affect his mental health, such as the death or serious illness of a close family member, divorce, or the birth of a sibling. Such events can feel like trauma to a child, causing varying degrees of anxiety and fear.

Children differ greatly in their resilience, in the ability to deal with stress and to integrate and bounce back from anxiety and fear. Research has shown that the biggest predictor of resilience is not some innate quality, but the support that families, teachers, and communities provide. While being in good physical and cognitive health can play a role, the support of consistent and thoughtful parents and of other protective adults will make the biggest difference in how a child copes with adversity.

Resilience is also strengthened by the many psychological and often unconscious methods that the average youngster has, even from the first months of life, for defending himself against anxiety. An infant who is frightened by a scary face will defend himself by looking away. An older child may simply pretend a frightening person is not there or will distract herself with happier thoughts. Psychological defenses are useful and necessary. Just as the immune system protects both adults and children from harmful bacteria, psychological defenses allow them to deal with the inevitable small setbacks in life (hurt feelings, fright, disappointment, and rejection) and to recover from major trauma (such as accident or divorce). Psychological defenses include exercising imagination and humor, taking some kind of action instead of remaining passive, denying danger, intellectualizing, ritualizing, and diverting one's thoughts. Thus, when a child seems to be so overwhelmed by worry as to be unable to function properly (for example, unable to do schoolwork or sleep at night), parents might enlist one of these psychological processes to help him cope. They may, for instance, offer him the chance to divert his thoughts by reading a book together or watching a movie. Just as one's immune system can go out of control, a child's defenses, especially denial or intellectualizing, may also do so. They may become so entrenched that they prevent her from confronting and dealing with real problems. A child facing an intimidating test, for example, may, instead of preparing for it, pretend that she has mastered the subject and that everything is fine. Although you and her family may try to help her come to terms with her underlying anxiety and cope with reality, it may be necessary to call in a therapist.

Emotional and behavioral problems have recognizable patterns, but each child's difficulties are unique. They reflect his own life story—his strengths and vulnerabilities, his history of burdens and gifts. Thus, children respond to similar traumas in very different ways. For one child, the birth of a sibling is a mild annoyance or even an exciting opportunity. For another, it is a moment of crisis that makes her feel betrayed and angry. During divorce, some children and adolescents find a way of navigating between their two parents and are able to sustain their relationships with both. For others, the marital stresses and arguments that precede divorce and the final breakup deeply shake their trust in one or both parents. They may become angry, depressed, and inattentive. They may struggle in school or take risky, destructive actions outside it.

Part of healthy development is a child's growing ability to understand what upsets her—to recognize her internal anxieties and stresses and to use this information to guide her thoughts and behavior. Parents and educators play an important role in helping a child understand normal difficulties and the occasional serious upsets, understand that painful feelings are part of life, and see their connection with events, hopes, desires, and relationships. Remember that even children who seem remarkably fortunate may be worried under the surface. At times they may feel more threatened and bothered than they would like others to know, even more than they know themselves. When a real crisis occurs for such a child, his facade may crumble quickly. Children who are more secure allow others to see that they are upset. They can reach out for help and can cope with their problems; they don't feel it is necessary to push them aside.

For a child with short-term and mild difficulties, consistent, thoughtful, calm care will help her develop the emotional skills to deal with these and future difficulties; but for a child whose problems are more troubling, loving care and time are not enough.

More than ten percent of children will have a behavioral, psychiatric, or developmental difficulty during their school years. These include learning problems, overactivity, depression, phobias, eating difficulties, and a host of other worries and dysfunctions. These problems may last a short time, fading as quickly as they emerged, or they may interfere with learning, friendships, and personal happiness. They can erode self-esteem, undermine a child's ability to achieve, and may ultimately require psychiatric help.

When a child's emotional problems persist for months or years, interfering with life at home or in school, they are often diagnosed with a mental illness, which can cause pain and suffering to both child and family and can threaten a child's life as severely as some medical conditions. As with some medical conditions, there is a genetic component related to certain mental illnesses, such as schizophrenia, autism, attentional problems, depression, and tic syndromes. Environmental factors can trigger a genetic response in a child who has a genetic vulnerability to a mental illness. As a result, the signs and symptoms of the illness begin to manifest and she loses the ability to regulate her behavior appropriately and needs psychiatric help.

Mental illness is not a parent's fault, but parents can alleviate or exacerbate it depending on their response to their child. When a child's behavior changes sharply, parents often do not know how to handle it—whether to ignore it, to care for the child in a special way, or to scold him or her. They wonder whether the behavior is a symptom of a serious problem. If they suspect that it may be due to a mental illness or disorder, they may wonder if they are responsible. Because of this feeling, exacerbated by the undeserved stigma of mental illness, they may hesitate to acknowledge the problem.

Since there are a lot of unknown factors involving mental disturbances, having a child with one is not only distressing but frustrating to parents. They may frequently turn to teachers and other caring adults in their children's lives for guidance and help in determining how "normal" the behaviors are within the childcare or school setting. In fact, early childhood and school years are often key times for mental health issues to come to light. In this chapter we aim to give you some insight into children's mental problems. We will talk about how to recognize the symptoms of developmental disorders that may arise in preschool and in school, how to find help for a child, and how to help parents deal with their own feelings.

Recognizing Symptoms of Disturbance

There are common behaviors that parents and caregivers see throughout childhood, such as temper tantrums for two-year-olds, separation worries on entering day care, a period of bed-wetting after an upsetting event like a bad accident, arguments when there is a lot of pressure at school, or preoccupation with appearance in adolescence. Several factors make it hard to know whether these problems are symptoms of serious disturbance. For example, about 25 percent of all mothers with a four-year-old boy will report that he is overly active. Preschoolers have a tiring combination of energy, mobility, and verbosity, and almost every child will seem overactive in certain situations. Since some families are much more tolerant than others of an ebullient child's constant questioning, chatter, and fidgeting, it is not possible to zero in on exactly how much activity in a four-year-old is too much and how much may reflect a real disturbance.

Another factor that makes it difficult to judge a child's mental health is her parents' expectations of what she should be like. As a child grows, she may change from being quiet and introspective to become suddenly rambunctious. Common quirks and difficulties may appear ominous but only because parents have certain hopes for their child's behavior. In reality, parents should expect such moments or even changes in their child's personality due in part to their rapid development during childhood.

Some symptoms reflect mild interferences with a child's healthy functioning and adaptation to stress, and often he can right himself with patience from his caregivers. When a problem arises gradually and fades over a week or two, most parents recognize that some problems are transient, and children have a right to their symptoms and bad periods. Pediatricians may sometimes suggest not treating minor illnesses and instead giving a child a day or two for his physical resiliency and immune system to bring him back to health. Similarly, by remaining calm,

affectionate, and engaged, without too much personal distress, caregivers can give a child time for his emotions to settle down. Making a big deal about something can reinforce its seriousness in a child's mind, thus increasing his anxiety level.

Most problems that children experience are either just part of the normal challenges of life or result from a period of transition or increased stress. For example, about 10 percent of all children exhibit some sort of nervous habit (tics, nail biting, nose picking) at some point in the first years of school. Everyone has good and bad days, good and bad periods. A child can become clingy and immature for no apparent reason, and begin acting more independently after a surge in maturation.

Children learn coping skills during challenging times with the help of parents who are warm and affectionate and resist overreacting. Teachers play an important role by providing students with a steady, calming presence and by teaching children strategies for dealing with challenges.

Symptoms of children's mental illness are varied and complex, as is their normal development. (For more on understanding development, see Chapter 1.) In fact, some symptoms manifest as delayed development. For example, a child may speak much later than normal or be slower in her intellectual development. Other symptoms are reflected in patterns of regulation or organization, such as when a child has trouble staying still, paying attention, or maintaining normal sleep patterns. Difficulty in the development of a basic competence, such as the ability to form loving, reciprocal social relations, can be another indicator.

Lines of development are useful in charting how a child is doing compared with other children. They also suggest the many different, concurrent processes that take place within a child as she grows, and the range of psychiatric, developmental, and emotional problems she may face. There appear to be inborn forces, both biological and neurological, that help keep developmental lines in motion. If a child seems stuck or derailed, or if development slows down or becomes distorted, therapists can work with him and his parents to identify what may be impeding or interfering with his functioning. They will do a developmental diagnosis to help a family understand when and why a problem may emerge and learn how to help a child regain the momentum he needs to move ahead. For most children, once these impediments are recognized and dealt with, the child's normal, inborn maturational forces will help him move back into a healthier course of development.

For young children, symptoms resulting from stress tend to affect many areas of functioning, and the developmental difficulties of very young children are often global. They may have physical problems (lack of growth, diarrhea, stomach pains) alongside emotional difficulties (irritability, anxiety, temper outbursts). As children grow older, their problems usually become localized to one area, such as bodily functions, emotions, behavior, or thinking. An older child may become depressed or overly excitable, steal, lie, and disobey authority, or be frightened by new situations, avoid groups, and generally feel overwhelmed. A child may have trouble with reading or math, or simply dawdle, unable to attend to schoolwork or homework.

Some children's emotional problems are mostly inwardly focused. They may be sad, moody, anxious, and unable to enjoy life's pleasures.

Others manifest outwardly. They disrupt family or school life by being overactive, impulsive, and disobedient. Or a child's problems cut across their inner and outer worlds, including feelings and thoughts as well as behavior. Their confusion about their thoughts and feelings results in behaviors that may concern those around them.

When parents recognize that their child's symptoms are serious and suspect that she has crossed the line from transient upset to persistent distress, they may worry and may delay finding suitable help to diagnose and suggest treatment for their child. If a child's problems seem serious and are protracted, caregivers should listen to their worries and seek help as soon as possible from a mental health professional. Further, trusted educators who care for children, observe them closely, and see them around other children are invaluable in guiding families to mental health evaluations and resources.

Major disturbances include serious attention deficit hyperactivity disorder (ADHD), autism spectrum disorder, obsessive-compulsive disorder, and depression. In the course of evaluating an individual child's problems, those who treat children do not like to use diagnostic labels too early but prefer to wait and see how things unfold. There comes a moment, however, when a child's difficulties crystallize in a persistent pattern of symptoms, and a specific diagnosis can help guide treatment. At such times, the use of a diagnostic term is not labeling a child invidiously, but is a way to help explain his troubles to him and those around him, and to direct his treatment. Some children even find comfort in knowing that there is a name for what is bothering them and that other people have undergone and coped with similar difficulties.

Labeling a child's mental health signs and symptoms with a diagnosis helps her and her family learn to understand the illness and can also guide her treatment and give her access to free programs and benefits.

Developmental Disturbances

Minor problems are commonly part of normal physical and behavioral development. At least 5 percent of children are born with some physical birth defect, and of those, most are very minor. There may also be small anomalies in the development of a baby's nervous system that can place a child at risk for common behavioral, learning, or emotional difficulties. The major disorders of development result from impairment in the unfolding of such basic competencies as social relations, language, and intellectual skills.

Most babies naturally smile and look at their parents and caregivers. They seem prewired to be socially engaged and engaging. But there are babies who, from the first months of life, seem apathetic and hard to engage, turn away or look through their parents, and fail to warm up. These babies become a greater worry for parents if they reach nine or twelve months and clearly seem to lag behind more outgoing children. Sometimes these delays are caused by a hearing impairment, sometimes they indicate a normally quiet child, and other times, they may be an indicator of a major developmental disorder.

Children with intellectual disability are sometimes identified at birth because of associated physical problems or signs. For instance, Down syndrome is often suspected based on its distinctive facial appearance and is confirmed by chromosome tests. Other intellectual disabilities are diagnosed by laboratory tests performed on all newborns, such as PKU (an inborn error of metabolism that can be mitigated by a special diet) or hypothyroidism (low levels of thyroid hormone). Children who are born very premature and quite small are at high risk for neurological problems in their first months; they may have bleeding in the brain because of their fragile blood vessels or may develop breathing problems. These medical problems also place a child at risk for later intellectual disability, but many very small infants, even with such difficulties, go on to develop well, especially if they go home to well-functioning families. Other forms of intellectual disability become apparent to families only during the first months or years of life, as a child shows delays in achieving such skills as walking and speaking.

The majority of children with intellectual disabilities are only somewhat behind typical children in their language, abstract thinking, and motor skills. If an average IQ is about 100, these children may have IQs in the 60s and similarly slow development in adaptive skills (self-care, communication, socialization). Only a small percentage of children with intellectual disability have clearly defined biological or organic causes for their problems and function in the more severely impaired range with IQs in the 30s and 40s.

The ultimate level of independence and adaptation that any child with intellectual disability achieves depends a great deal on the child's experience, not just on inborn brain capacity. Loving acceptance in the family, engagement with peers and others in the community, suitable education, and opportunities for recreation and achievement make enormous differences in their lives. Indeed, the quality of an intellectually disabled child's social life, motivation, and self-esteem may make as much or more difference in life than would ten or fifteen points on an IQ test.

The most serious disorder of development is autism spectrum disorder (ASD), a condition that was identified nearly eighty years ago and that has since been seen throughout the world in every nation and demographic. Children with ASD have pervasive difficulties in every sphere of development, particularly in social relations and communication. Many are also intellectually disabled, and about half never speak. These children have a range of unusual behaviors, such as repetitive movements, and they find it difficult to play imaginatively. (See "Understanding Autism Spectrum Disorder," pages 30.) In its most severe form, ASD is relatively uncommon, affecting perhaps one child in a thousand. But milder developmental disorders produce some of the same types of dysfunction in social relations and language, and perhaps one child in two hundred may have some signs and symptoms similar to those of ASD. Autism spectrum disorder is a biologically based developmental disorder; it is not caused by a child's upbringing. However, a child's experiences in her family, special education, and therapeutic treatments may, as with intellectual disabilities, make a great difference in the outcome.

The most frequent developmental disorders are probably those related to language and communication. Some children speak earlier than others, and some speak abnormally late. Children who are still not speaking by the age of two and a half deserve thorough evaluation and treatment. At times, such delayed development of speech is the result of a sensory problem, such as deafness or recurrent middle ear infections, or being deprived of opportunities to engage in talking. For most children, the cause of delayed speech is not known.

Problems of the Preschool and School Years

Three-year-old children are imaginative, outgoing, and ebullient; they are fun to watch at play and eager to have an adult join as a partner in the game. At this age, they remember what they did yesterday and look forward to tomorrow's trip to the bakery or the zoo. They understand, or at least seem to understand, virtually everything you say to them, and they talk about life in sentences and short paragraphs.

A preschool child who seems to be developing on track can still demonstrate problems in the areas of emotional, intellectual, and physical achievement.

A three-year-old can worry constantly or be overactive, inattentive, and disruptive. Another can resist playing with other children or struggle to make friends. Sometimes a child may have trouble recounting her experiences, planning, or waiting. There are many different diagnostic labels for these troubles. A child with the diagnosis of ADHD is overactive, inattentive, and impulsive. A child with an anxiety disorder has fears beyond those appropriate for his age. A child who is diagnosed with oppositional defiant disorder disagrees with his parents about everything, fights back, and resists accepting the normal rules of social life.

The behavioral signs of emotional or psychological difficulty in an older child vary widely and may include severe temper tantrums, severe aggressiveness or hyperactivity, lying and stealing, withdrawn or isolated behavior, school refusal, excessive fears, and lack of motivation or decreased enjoyment of activities. In the school years, emotional problems may manifest themselves as academic difficulties. Sometimes a student who has learning disabilities in the areas of reading, spelling, or arithmetic has other symptoms as well, such as ADHD.

When a child has trouble in school and fails to keep up with his peers, he is at risk for other behavioral or emotional problems. He may suffer from low self-esteem or depression and continual worrying. He may avoid school or act out to mask or distract himself from his troubles. (For more on how schools treat learning disabilities, see Chapter 7.) If a child's behavior changes sharply or development does not seem normal, parents should consult their pediatrician. If the doctor identifies a problem, he may recommend further evaluation with a mental health professional to clarify its nature and severity and decide whether the child needs psychological or educational help.

Childhood Tics

Tics are common in childhood, especially in second and third grades. A tic can be eye blinking, nose puckering, grimacing, or other small, fast muscular contractions.

Most young children are unaware that they have a tic. Although older children grow aware of these movements, they do not know why they happen. A child will describe a funny feeling, like an itch, in a part of her body that she can ease by making a small movement. Tics generally come and go over a period of weeks to months, and a new tic may replace an old one. For most people, simple childhood tics go away, leaving no trace.

Some children, however, develop many tics of the face and body and may, in addition, start to make noises or sounds (phonic or vocal tics). These can disturb other students in school and their family at home. Children with the most severe tic problems may have six to ten different types of muscle and vocal tics and emit them many times a minute for most of the day. A child can have a range of ever-changing tics that last for many months—a condition known as Tourette syndrome. Children diagnosed with this disorder often report that a strange feeling in a part of their body tells them that a tic is about to occur and that the tic then lessens that feeling. Although Tourette syndrome is visible, and vocal tics can be especially disruptive and embarrassing, it can be managed and a child can develop into a successful adult with the support of understanding families, teachers, and friends.

Obsessions and Compulsions

Around the age of ten or eleven, children normally enjoy hobbies, collecting, and learning the rules of games. For some children, however, their patterns of organizing ideas and objects become excessive and develop into a behavioral, or obsessive-compulsive, disorder. A child with this disorder may compulsively do the same thing over and over, such as washing her hands, lining up toys in her room, or checking to be sure that she has not broken something. The child also begins to experience irrational fears that manifest in her behavior. She may spend hours in the shower using up bars of soap, be unable to move through a doorway because she cannot step over the threshold, hoard unnecessary string or paper, or feel too worried to throw something away. Eventually this disorder comes to control a child's life. Parents may be forced to help with their child's rituals, rather than deny them or force him to ignore them, to keep him from feeling too scared.

Many children with Tourette syndrome also have obsessive-compulsive disorder. Both conditions seem to reflect a genetic vulnerability that is transmitted within a family. Although a good deal is known about the interaction between genetic and environmental factors leading to disorders such as Tourette or debilitating obsessions and compulsions, we still do not know why some children succumb to them.

Depression

Since the 1970s, psychologists have recognized that children and adolescents may become depressed. A child feels blue, cannot enjoy normal pleasures like parties and friendships, is tearful, loses weight because he finds no pleasure in eating, has trouble falling or staying asleep, and may think about suicide. Although childhood depression most typically emerges closer to adolescence, it is not unheard of to see evidence of depression in children as young as 6 or 7. It can be difficult to identify the difference between the normal ebbs and flows of a child's moodiness and bouts of sadness with a more serious—but treatable—indication of depression. If you are concerned, try to ask the family about issues that affect sleeping, eating, and trouble concentrating.

During adolescence, perhaps one-quarter of all girls and almost as many boys suffer some level of depression for periods of a few weeks or months. Depression can become more serious and sustained and lead to a range of other problems: social withdrawal, school failure, and real attempts at suicide. Surprisingly, even adolescents who are not depressed have thoughts about suicide or actually try to hurt themselves. Thus, depression in adolescence, when a child may be naturally disposed to suicidal thoughts, is especially serious.

Some situations make particular types of disturbance more likely. When a child is exposed to violence at home or is abused or neglected, she is likely to feel anxious and depressed and to be inattentive and impulsive. Children raised in families where there is drug or alcohol abuse, or whose parents are involved in crime, are also at high risk of substance abuse, disruptive behavior, and later crime. Exposure to violence in war- and crime-plagued areas may lead children to develop post-traumatic stress disorder, in which they become highly sensitive to danger, startle easily, have flashbacks to the violent situation, feel somewhat numb to normal experiences, and are generally distracted and less able to engage in school.

Seeking Help for a Child

If you recognize problematic behaviors in a child, raise the issue to the child's parents and suggest that they find help. It is important to find professionals who are qualified to evaluate a child's behavior and development and to help assess her need for different forms of therapy, psychotropic medications, or even hospitalization.

Sometimes it is apparent by the end of a child's first year in school that there are some mental health issues needing to be addressed, but often the earliest symptoms become clear only in retrospect. When a child does develop symptoms, they can be dramatic—developing over a few days or weeks—or subtle, developing more slowly. A sad, withdrawn child may strike her parents as just quiet, even refreshingly undemanding, until they realize that she is failing in school, tearful, and without friends.

The first step in seeking help for a child is to recognize that she is suffering—that her development has gone off track.

Many schools have counselors or psychologists who can provide an evaluation. Parents can also consult their child's pediatrician, who is medically trained to understand each child as a whole person. When symptoms persist or are impairing a child's behavior, a more specialized evaluation from a child psychologist (a nonmedical specialist in child development and treatment) or a child and adolescent psychiatrist (a medical specialist in the area of children's emotional and psychiatric problems) may be warranted. These professionals have advanced training both in the assessment of normal development and in conducting diagnostic assessments.

Anxious Nina

As an infant and toddler, Nina was so lovely that people stopped on the street to smile at her. She spoke in charming phrases by eighteen months and was a sweet little girl at two years. When her baby brother, Jason, was born, she seemed thrilled and told all her friends about "my baby." She would run to console Jason when he cried and bring a clean diaper when their mother was caring for him. Nina was especially helpful when Jason had to have minor surgery on his ear for a birth defect. She liked to bring him things to cheer him up but would get very worried whenever she saw a bloody discharge on the bandage that covered his ear for a few weeks.

Nina was such a competent child that everyone was surprised when, at age three, she became miserable on the first day of nursery school. She clung to her mother, begged to go home, and wept until her eyes were red. Both parents accompanied Nina to nursery school during the first days, taking turns being with her, but to no avail. After a few weeks, she had her first toilet accident and wet her pants. Then her parents realized that Nina was holding back her stools. Her stomach began to hurt, and every two or even three days, she would have a painful bowel movement and so began to fear these events even more.

During the next six months, Nina's whole personality seemed to shift. Her smile dimmed, and she would grimace or hold her lips tight together. She no longer enjoyed playing with her dinosaurs and dressing up in costumes. She seemed distant and preoccupied. On some nights, she would awaken with a nightmare. Her parents talked with their pediatrician, who found nothing physically wrong and suggested they consult with a child psychiatrist. Dr. Matthews first met Nina's parents for an extended discussion of her development, current problems, and family. They described Jason's high energy and how he had taken over the family with his tricks and enthusiasm.

Dr. Matthews then spent several sessions with Nina, who had just turned four. During their first meeting, Nina's mother stayed and watched quietly, helping to make her daughter feel more comfortable in the doctor's office. At the next sessions, Nina was able to be alone with Dr. Matthews, but she checked the waiting room a few times to be sure her mother was still there. Dr. Matthews allowed Nina to take the lead in talking and playing. She spoke softly about being worried. "I have thoughts on my mind" was the longest explanation she offered for her sadness. Among his questions, Dr. Matthews asked about her stomachaches. Nina said that they were "all better," but the doctor could see her wince occasionally. Nina gravitated to a box of toy figures and cars, then to a dollhouse in which she placed various family members. She worked calmly in her play, bringing Dr. Matthews into the narrative she was creating about a tense moment as mother is making supper and the baby throws up.

Over the next few sessions, Nina played out various scenarios about family life, the arrival of a new baby, trips to the country, and airplane rides. Often, the "nice family" would have a sudden change of fortune. Someone would get very sick and have to be rushed to the hospital, or a car would crash into the family standing at the side of the road. The little girl in the family—clearly a stand-in for Nina herself—was sometimes angry and even "wicked." She would throw objects from the top of the dollhouse. At times, the doll got hurt: her finger or head was cut, and she was badly injured by a "dynamite bomb." Dr. Matthews would play alongside Nina and gently ask questions or elaborate the dialogue. Mostly, he wished to convey that she could explore her own feelings and tell the story on her mind in her own way.

After two months, Dr. Matthews felt that he was better able to understand Nina's inner world and the transformation that occurred in her with the birth of Jason and his surgery. With her effort to be a very good girl, she had covered over her natural angry feelings about sensing she had been displaced in her parents' life. Inside, though, she felt furious, especially with her father, who was thrilled at having a son. "They play basketball," Nina would say about Jason, both directly and in playing with the toy figures. "They are just alike." When Jason got his "ear cut"—actually, the ear was only slightly reshaped—Nina thought that maybe her thoughts about hurting him had caused the injury. This thought scared her, though part of her felt that he got what he deserved for displacing her.

Dr. Matthews could appreciate the rage underlying Nina's depression and anxiety. He felt that she was worried that her anger would hurt her mother, just as it had hurt Jason. Her inside world—her mind and then her body—became filled with frightening fantasies. In simple language, Dr. Matthews shared some of his thoughts through the play. He would comment on the angry feelings in the girl figure and on the fears that Mommy and Daddy would be furious if they knew what she was thinking. He helped Nina to express her own worries more openly and then actually to share her conviction that she had to be very good because being angry was so dangerous. They discussed her jealousy and her well-justified annoyance at her father for making such a big deal about Jason.

During these months, Dr. Matthews also met with Nina's mother and father every other week to talk about their feelings and thoughts. Slowly, they were able to discuss Nina's experiences in the family. Dad appreciated that he was too interested in Jason and "boy stuff" and that this must have hurt Nina, whom he adored. As the family became more aware of Nina's feelings, and as she was able to express her needs, anger, and confusion more clearly, they rediscovered their old pleasures in being together. Dad and Nina went for long walks in the nearby park, talked about the flowers, and had a nice time buying jelly doughnuts. Ten months after she had first played at Dr. Matthews's office, Nina simply sat down on the toilet one day and had a bowel movement, without thinking much about pain.

A psychiatrist will meet with the parents and child, will gather information from the school and the pediatrician, and will conduct specialized psychological and medical tests to carefully evaluate a complicated problem. Understanding a child's difficulties requires a full understanding of his strengths and competencies, as well as the specific symptoms. It means knowing the child's whole life history and current situation at home and in school.

Evaluation and discussion can be therapeutic in and of themselves. They may help both a child and her family understand better what is happening, when problems really arose, and how each family member is reacting. These insights alone sometimes lead to changes in a child's world that may improve her state of mind.

Therapy for Children

For children with serious problems, there are many approaches to treatment and care. In psychotherapy, a child can explore his feelings. Other professionals, such as social workers or child psychologists, may offer specific guidance to parents and teachers or teach a child more effective behaviors, such as alternatives to throwing a temper tantrum, or ways to resist a compulsion. Special education can help children with reading and other school problems. (See Chapter 7.) Some children will benefit from group therapy; others may need to be in a special class or school.

Child psychiatrists and psychologists working with a very young child often encourage her to draw pictures of what is on her mind or to play with dolls and other toys they keep in the office. Because of their limited capacity for introspection, the elementary level of their language skills, and their likely inhibitions, children often express themselves more elaborately and ultimately more effectively through nonverbal means than through speaking. In this way, a child like Nina (see "Anxious Nina," pages 164–165) can successfully work through potentially destructive symptoms.

Psychotropic Medication

Today, medications are formulated to help children with specific types of psychiatric or behavioral problems. The most widely used are called stimulants, which improve a child's attention and reduce impulsivity in ADHD. Other medications have proven effective in reducing tics, helping with obsessions and compulsions, reducing anxiety, and

alleviating depression. Children with the most severe disorders, such as psychosis or autism spectrum disorder, may need to take highly potent medications for years; these drugs can make the conditions more manageable but do not remove them. Some people, unfortunately, receive no benefit from the medications that are currently available.

Any decision to use medication must be made after a thorough evaluation of all the factors that may have led to a child's problems and of all the possible remedies, including potential benefits and short- and long-term side effects of any medication being considered. These benefits and effects will vary according to the age of the child. The decisions to start a medication and to stop it must be based on a child's overall development, not just on the presence of a symptom, but medications can be an effective part of treatment. (See "Impulsive Brad," on the next page.) The recommendation that a family consider medication for a child should come from pediatricians and mental health professionals, not from educators.

Impulsive Brad

As a baby, Brad ran before he walked, and after his first step, never stopped. In day care, he took what he wanted and bumped into the other children on the way. At home, he had one accident after another. One day his parents were terrified to see him run into the street and be thrown into the air by an oncoming car. The screeching brakes were engraved in their memories for years, and any time they heard a car squeal, they would recall their panic. Brad suffered a concussion and a fractured arm. He left the hospital bruised and with a cast and was—for a short while—less impulsive and quieter than before.

Soon after Brad started school, his teachers complained that he kept popping in and out of his seat—he could not control his behavior. His handwriting was poor, and he daydreamed while the other children read aloud. He, in turn, felt annoyed to be always the object of their criticism. The school psychologist tested Brad as he entered second grade. The results were encouraging. His intellectual abilities were solidly above average, although his academic skills were lagging behind. The psychologist documented his distractibility, impulsivity, and tendency to blurt out answers before thinking. She felt these findings were consistent with the clinical observation of attention deficit hyperactivity disorder.

The school psychologist and special resource teacher worked out an educational program for Brad to help him focus on work, learn to plan ahead, and develop more internal controls over his activity. (For more on this special education process, see pages 112–117.) When Brad was taught verbally and rewarded for success, he learned to persevere and to organize himself.

Around this time, Brad's pediatrician met with his parents to discuss other ways of helping him. The doctor suggested that it might be worthwhile to try a stimulant medication. She asked the boy's teachers to use a scale to rate Brad's behavior in school, and the parents did the same thing about their observations at home. She then started Brad on medication at a low dose to lessen the chance of a poor reaction. During the next several weeks, the dose of medication was slowly moved up to a usual therapeutic range.

The pediatrician, the parents, and the teachers followed Brad's behavior and also watched for side effects. The results of the medication, in combination with the behavioral and educational interventions, were impressive. Brad was far more cooperative with the resource teacher, began to take pride in his work, and was able to settle down for longer periods at home. His teachers scolded him less, and his parents were not yelling at him as much. The house was so quiet one afternoon that Brad's mother, feeling that something was wrong, went looking for her son. He was in his room quietly absorbed in a picture book.

A school-age child who has to take a medication may feel that it means he is "bad" or defective. This impression may be reinforced if his siblings and friends do not take medications or if he must take a dose in school, as is often the case with stimulants. Alternatively, some children assume that medication will take care of all their problems and adopt a passive attitude, blaming any further behavioral difficulties on an unhelpful drug. A child who feels "trapped" into taking a pill she never asked for may refuse to take it, avoid her doses, or merely pretend to take the pill and then spit it out. The more a child is engaged in the process of choosing her treatment, the more likely she will be to follow it. It often helps a school-age child to be in the office while her doctors and parents consult and then have an opportunity to talk privately to the doctor. A child who gains a sense of safety, care, and openness is more likely to participate wholeheartedly in her treatment.

Helping Families Deal with Their Own Feelings

Parents who are told that their child has a serious emotional, behavioral, or psychiatric disorder usually feel a mix of emotions. On one side, they are relieved to learn that the behavior that has troubled them and possibly frightened their child fits into a pattern or diagnosis and is treatable. On the other hand, the gravity of the news may fill them with despair and disappointment. They may wish to ignore the severity of the diagnosis as a way of protecting themselves from those feelings. Or the diagnosis may reignite parents' worries about whether they are in any way to blame for their child's difficulties. If parents of a child in your class express these feelings, remind them that not even the advantages of an intact family, good schooling, and a robust genetic background can fully immunize a child against certain kinds of serious trouble.

Any parent of a child with a serious psychiatric disorder finds it extremely difficult to adjust his or her thinking and expectations. It is a task demanding strength, compassion, and sacrifice from every member of the family, and may result in emotional stress for siblings as well. Sometimes the adjustment is so difficult that families come apart; at other times, families come together closer than before.

Good care is essential, of course, to allow a child to more easily express his needs when he is upset and to show his symptoms. If you have a student with a mental health issue, make sure to appreciate him as a whole person, not just a set of behavioral or emotional symptoms. And understand these symptoms in the context of his strengths and how he is functioning in all spheres of life, as well as in relation to the supports and stresses in his family, school, and community.

Thoughtful developmental diagnosis is not a matter of finding a single label, but is instead a short story about a child with many facets. Labels often carry a stigma, so accepting the seriousness of mental illness and understanding the deep impact mental problems have on a family is a long process. It is important to see a child's problems not just as a diagnosis but as a part of the person he is.

Building Resilience in Children and Families

This chapter has touched on some of the challenging mental health issues that can arise with children in early childhood and throughout the lifespan. Whether challenges arise from developmental delays and disorders or other external situations, the chances are you will encounter children who face some adversity in their lives.

Research over the last decades has taught us much about the impact of adversity and trauma on children's developing brains, on their ability to learn, and on the potential long-term impact of adverse childhood experiences on a person's future health, wellness, and success.

However, more recent learnings have pointed science in an encouraging and less deterministic direction. Research has shown that positive supports from caring adults can go a long way toward mitigating the impact of childhood stressors. Some of those buffers come directly from the influence of teachers and the school community that you help create for your children and their families.

In addition, studies have demonstrated the impact that literacy and place-based learning can have on creating those positive balances that offset trauma. Introducing the value of storytelling (through reading, oral language, word play, and songs) will help build an understanding of narrative that can bolster a child's sense of identity. Celebrating the place in which you live can foster a sense of belonging and pride in community. All of these steps will help provide a child with tools that build lifelong resilience.

Mental health issues in children are not uncommon. Some may be mild and transient, while others may be more serious and lifelong. Some may arise from brain development or genetics, and others may be a result of trauma. Because children respond to their own unique experiences in their own way, it can be challenging to help them navigate difficult times. You can provide them with a steady and calming presence and teach them strategies to deal with challenges.

Understanding some of the more common mental illnesses can help you know when to involve parents and when to suggest that they seek psychiatric help. Stress and trauma can slow development or affect other areas of functioning. When a child's symptoms become persistent, it may be appropriate to suggest the family meet with a mental health professional.

Developmental disorders may result from a genetic or congenital cause and often involve delays in social, language, and intellectual skills. The range of severity means that some children with developmental disabilities may become completely independent as adults and others may require lifelong care.

Emotional and psychological difficulties in preschool and school-age children may manifest as behavioral or academic problems. Some mental illnesses that may show up in childhood include attention deficit hyperactivity disorder, tics, obsessions and compulsions, and depression. Identifying children whose development has gone off track because of a mental illness may be challenging for a preschool teacher, but helping parents get treatment for their child and deal with their own preconceptions about mental illness can be invaluable to the success of the child. Some children find therapy is an effective treatment, while others may need medication. Getting help for these children as early as possible is important for achieving the best possible outcome.

Many children face some form of adversity in their lives. These challenges can affect them emotionally and academically. However, the loving support of caring adults can offset these difficulties. Children who receive positive support are most likely to build resilience that will last into adulthood.

Photo Credits

Photos ©: 1: Weekend Images Inc./Getty Images; 3: FatCamera/E+/Getty Images; 12: Halfpoint/Getty Images; 18: RichVintage/Getty Images; 21: monkeybusinessimages/Getty Images; 27: fatihhoca/Getty Images; 35: Anna Pekunova/Getty Images; 39: Chris Bernard/Getty Images; 44: hunnicutt2004/Getty Images; 47: damircudic/Getty Images; 50: shironosov/Getty Images; 52: FatCamera/Getty Images; 58: PeopleImages/Getty Images; 65: Weekend Images Inc./Getty Images; 67: Ariel Skelley/Getty Images; 75: Ariel Skelley/Getty Images; 97: Westend61/Getty Images; 108: sturti/Getty Images; 116: Jovanmandic/Getty Images; 120: sturti/Getty Images; 125: Ariel Skelley/Getty Images; 128: FatCamera/Getty Images; 139: kali9/Getty Images; 143: FatCamera/Getty Images; 146: Igor Emmerich/Cultura RM Exclusive/Getty Images; 167: FatCamera/Getty Images. All other photos © Shutterstock.com.

Index

abstract thinking, 7
academic skills, 102
adaptation and skill mastery,
    8, 9–10
ADHD (attention deficit
    hyperactivity disorder),
    13, 160
  a case study, 168
  and medication, 166–167
adversity
  coping with, 152
  effects of, 170
advocating for a child, 118–119
age, chronological vs.
    developmental, 99
aggressive behavior, 110, 132,
    134–137, 160
  a case study, 136
American College Testing
    assessment (ACT), 111
anger, 134–135
  a case study, 164–165
anxiety, 59, 160, 163. *See also*
    separation anxiety
  a case study, 164–165
  coping strategies, 152–153
  over tests, 111–112
  in preschoolers, 129
  in school-age children, 131–132
anxiety disorder, 160
assessments
  developmental, 11
  mental health, 15, 160
  of preschoolers, 105
assimilation, defined, 6
athletics in school, 104–105
attention deficit hyperactivity
    disorder. *See* ADHD
autism spectrum disorder (ASD),
    30, 59, 159
  and medication, 167
axons, 20

behavioral disorders, 161
behavioral problems, 13, 16, 152
  and medication, 166–167
  seeking help for, 163
"best friends", 147
bilingual environment, 68
Binet, Alfred, 6
biological systems, 5
birth defects, physical, 157
books, 87–89, 90, 92. *See also*
    reading; reading aloud to
    children; reading aloud by
    children
  picture, 92
  for preschoolers, 92
  and television, 92
  for toddlers, 88
  types, 88, 90
brain development
  critical periods, 22–23
  environmental influence,
    19, 20–21
  optimizing, 25
  and stimulation, 22–23
  in utero, 19
brain development, 19–25

central nervous system, 40
child development field, 1–4
child psychiatrist, 163
child psychologist, 163, 164–165, 166
child study team. *See* PPT (planning
    and placement team)
children, as individuals, 16
clinical evaluation, need for, 15
cognitive development, 6–7, 131
cognitive self and emotional self, 121
cognitive skills, 93, 121
communication. *See also* language;
    language development
  and cultural differences, 108
  in first year, 68–69

  and friendship, 143
  nonverbal, 66–67, 68, 85
  persuasive, 73
  in preschool years, 74–77
  in second year, 69–71
  between teacher and
    family, 108
  in third year, 72–75
  verbal, 103
communication cues, 67–68
compulsions, 161
computer literacy, 92
computers, and children, 93
concrete operational stage of
    cognitive development, 7
convergent thinking, 58
coping skills, 152–153, 156
core competencies
crawling, 43
creativity, 57–58
critical periods, of brain
    development, 22–24
cross-modal perception, 85
crying, 67
cultural differences, and
    communication, 108
curiosity, 32

dangerous behavior, 146
daydreaming, 50–51
dendrites, 20
depression, 162–163
  a case study, 164–165
development areas, blending
    of, 46
development patterns,
    "normal", 15
development rates, differences
    in, 10–11, 25, 34, 106
development tips,
    preschool, 26
developmental age, 99–100

internalizing responsibility,
133–134, 148
interpreting a child's thoughts,
31–33

joint attention, 31–33

Kanner, Leo, 30
kindergarten, adjustments to,
100–101, 105
kindergarteners and first graders,
reading to, 86–87

language, 36. *See also*
communication
and bilingual environment, 68
first words, 69–70, 78
and grammar, 72–74
and "please", 73
and pronunciation, 74, 96
and reading, 96
sentence creation, 70–71,
75–76
and sounds, 67–68
stimulating, 68, 71
and understanding, 72–75
language development.
See also communication
and being read to, 85
and crying, 67
first words, 69–70, 78
first year, 68–69
influences of, 65–66
and passage of time, 72
sentence creation, 70–71
vocabulary, 70–71
learning disability(ies), 112–113, 160
advocating for children with,
118–119
and attention span, 115
defined, 113–114
identifying, 115
vs. learning difference, 116
overcoming, 119
parental involvement,
118–119
scope, 114

and self-esteem, 118
and success, 115
teaching children with, 118
"learning disabled" diagnosis, 117
learning process, 6, 93
left-handedness, 46–47
literacy, 79–80, 89, 102–103.
See also reading
literacy development, 89, 102–103
literacy milestones, 90

"make believe". *See* imaginary
play; pretending
manners, teaching to children,
73, 76–77
mathematics skills, 101, 104
mental growth, stages, 3
mental health
assessing, 15, 163, 166
factors that affect, 152
mental health disturbances,
157, 163
mental health professionals, 163
mental illness
affects on families, 169–170
diagnosis and examples of,
153–154
and genetics, 154
and response of parents, 154,
169–170
symptoms of, 156
milestones
literacy, 90
motor skills, 45
and variability among children,
10–11
writing, 90
mind, 27, 34
misbehavior, 109–110, 113
misinterpretation of actions, 33–34
motor coordination, and nerve
growth, 40–41
motor skills. *See also* fine motor
skills; gross motor skills;
voluntary movement
and computers, 93
development of, 39, 41–42

encouragement of, 48–49
milestones, 45
motivation to master, 43, 44
and nerve growth, 40–41
in newborns, 40–42
progression, 43, 46
reflexive, 40, 41
setbacks in developing, 48
voluntary, 41
myelin, 40–41

nature vs. nurture, 4–5
nerve cells, 19–20
nervous system, development, 19
neural network(s), 20–22
neurological problems, in
premature babies, 158
neurons, 19–21
neurotransmitters, 20
newborns
behavior patterns of, 122
and communication
emotions in, 122
reflexes in, 41
social interaction with, 124
temperament, 123–124
"normal" development patterns, 15
nursery rhymes, 83

"object permanence", 7
obsessive-compulsive disorder, 161
only children, 140
operational stage of cognitive
development, 7
oppositional defiant disorder, 160

paths of development, 11, 15
peers
comparison to, 94, 113, 130,
135, 160
interaction with, 98, 148–149
personality, defined, 123
persuasive communication, 73
phonics, 91
physical development, 16, 39
physical education, 104
Piaget, Jean, 3, 6–7, 17, 57, 143